The Ultimate Guide to
Fishing

igloobooks

igloobooks

Published in 2015
by Igloo Books Ltd
Cottage Farm
Sywell
NN6 0BJ
www.igloobooks.com

SHE001 0715
2 4 6 8 10 9 7 5 3 1
ISBN 978-1-78440-202-0

Text for Coarse Fishing John Bailey
Text for Fly Fishing Nick Hart
Text for Sea Fishing Jim O'Donnell

Front cover: main image © Mark Wragg / Getty Images,
br © Thinkstock / Getty Images
Back cover © Thinkstock / Getty Images

Printed and manufactured in China

CONTENTS

Coarse Fishing

INTRODUCTION

In Britain and mainland Europe, coarse fishing is the most popular form of fishing. The term coarse fishing refers to fishing for species other than those from the salmon and trout family using bait and spinners. Why is coarse fishing so popular? For a start, there is a whole range of exotic, desirable and different species that you will want to pursue. If you're a trout fisherman, you're limited to a couple of subspecies. Not so the coarse fisherman. There are at least a dozen types of fish that will keep you busy for every month of the year.

Coarse fishing will introduce you to a range of different skills. You might be trotting a river with a float, fishing a swim feeder on large stillwaters, stalking carp in the margins, fishing for chub with floating crust or working an artificial rubber fish around some lily beds for a summer pike. In short, if you're going to become the complete coarse fisherman, there are scores of different approaches, different skills and different types of fascination for you to master and enjoy.

There is also a whole variety of different water types. You might be interested in stillwaters, but these can be anything from tiny farm ponds to massive lakes and reservoirs. Then you have running water. Perhaps you're fishing a small stream or brook, perhaps a medium-sized river or maybe a watercourse as massive as the Thames or the Rhine. There are totally wild fisheries too, that exist despite, not because of, people. At the other end of the scale, lots of commercial fisheries have been created with diggers and stocked from lorries. There's nothing wrong with fisheries such as these. Often they're the best place to start coarse fishing, especially if you're unsure about your techniques.

The wise coarse fisherman will set different targets each and every season. Sometimes, it's tempting to fish only for carp. But I feel — as do most others — that every fish has its season. For example, pike are awesome in the winter. Tench and bream are super in the spring. Save your carp fishing for the summer and then enjoy the fall on barbel, chub and perch. There's a fish for every season and a different skill needed to catch it.

In short, if you want to be a coarse fisherman, you're embarking on an angling adventure that will consume your entire life!

COARSE FISH SPECIES

THE WATERS IN WHICH THEY LIVE, THE BAIT
AND THE METHODS USED TO CATCH THEM

In Britain and mainland Europe, there is a range of different species to pursue and enjoy. Remember, however, that all fish are wonderful works of nature. Enjoy them for their colours, their grace and their magnificent beauty. Small or large, it doesn't really matter. If you catch a pristine fish, makes sure that it goes back as unharmed as the moment it took your bait. All fish are pearls of nature. Try to keep them that way.

So let's take a look at our coarse fish species – from roach to eels, we are listing them in an approximate order of their popularity.

Roach

Heading the list is the roach. A good roach is probably around 1lb (0.4kg) in weight with a really good specimen being double this size. If you take a 3lb (1.4kg) roach, then it's the catch of a lifetime. You'll find roach throughout virtually all of Europe in both still and running waters – they have no real preference. They are equally laid back when it comes to baits. Maggots and casters are favourite, but they'll take sweetcorn, bread and worms with equal gusto. Probably, the very finest way of catching roach is on a float, especially on a river with a stick float or long trotting. On stillwaters, you'll need to use either a waggler float or a swim feeder in conjunction with a quiver tip.

A colossal river roach, weighing almost 3lb (1.4kg).

A fine example of a fully scaled common carp.

A massive river roach, weighing over 2lb (0.9kg).

This type of carp is usually called a ghost.

Carp

Next up we've got the carp. There are several different varieties of carp – most usually mirrors, commons and leathers. Mirrors have scattered scales, commons are fully scaled and leathers have no scales at all. A really good carp will weigh 20lb (9kg) and the fish of a lifetime will clock in at 30lb (13.5kg) or more. If you catch a 50lb (22.7kg) carp, then you're an angler to be reckoned with! You'll find carp in almost all stillwaters around Europe. They only really start to thin out in northern Scandinavia and parts of Ireland. Carp favour stillwaters and you'll catch them in farm ponds or vast reservoirs. However, you'll also find them in rivers and might be surprised at how fast a current they can cope with. Baits for carp tend to be quite specialised these days and most fish are caught on round, marblelike creations called boilies. Hard, dry, brown pellets are also popular. However, carp can still be caught on old favourites such as bread, luncheon meat, maggots and sweetcorn. Most carp are caught firmly on the bottom, often on a bolt rig. This is a heavy lead weight close to the hook that makes the carp bolt when it feels the weight. If the hook point is exposed, then the fish will hook itself. This is ideal for carp anglers who often fall asleep during a long session! Carp can also be caught stalking in the margins with a float. In fine weather, carp are keen to come to the surface and take food items. This is perhaps the most exciting way of catching them.

Pike

Pike are found in every pit, pond, stream or river throughout Europe. You'll even find them in the brackish margins of the Baltic Sea, where they thrive on the salt content and the vast food stocks that the Baltic provides. A big pike is considered to be about 20lb (9kg), but massive fish between 30 and 50lb (13.5 and 22.7kg) are waiting to be caught. Pike eat nothing but flesh – these heavily toothed predators will even devour waterfowl at certain times of the year. Because of their sharp teeth, you'll also need to fish for pike with a wire trace. Dead fish baits are an excellent way to catch pike. Try ordinary freshwater species, such as roach or small bream or sea fish such as herring and mackerel. You can also fish for pike with massive success using plugs, spinners and spoons. My personal favourites are single-hooked rubber fish. These look, feel and act as close to the real thing as you can get.

See the joy that fishing can bring! This magnificent pike has brightened up the day for two brothers.

Barbel

The barbel is a huge favourite across Europe. Generally, these are river fish where they prefer strong currents. A 10lb (4.5kg) barbel is an excellent trophy; if you catch a barbel of 15lb (6.8kg) or more, then you've truly got a catch of a lifetime. Barbel will eat pretty much everything. Favourite baits include boilies, luncheon meat, maggots, pellets, worms and small fish. I've even caught them on jelly babies and strips of anchovy! Most barbel are caught on the bottom, either using a leger weight or a swim feeder. However, the most spectacular and skilful way to catch barbel is on a float. With a float, you can trundle a bait through swim and make it look as natural as the real thing.

Ian Miller holds a fantastic early summer tench, weighing just over 10lb (4.4kg).

A magnificent, sleek river barbel.

Tench

Everyone loves tench. They are common fish, particularly in stillwaters. The tench is very much a fish of dawn and dusk, although you'll occasionally catch them during the day. They are mainly warm water fish, but you'll sometimes catch them in cooler weather. I target tench from May through to September. These fish are slow, cautious, choosy feeders. Maggots and casters are excellent bait, but they will also take boilies and pellets and you can try bread flake and worms. Tench are caught at range using swim feeders and small baits. Catch them on scaled-down carp tactics but, best of all, on the float. Nearly always you'll use a waggler float and fish at comparatively close range for these beautiful fish.

The sleek form of a fine tench. Notice the tiny scales and the piercing red eye.

Chub

Chub are common across Europe. They are almost exclusively river fish, just as the tench is almost exclusively a stillwater species. Chub and tench are similar in size, so catch a 5lb (2.2kg) fish and you've done well. A 7lb (3.2kg) fish is an excellent specimen and anything above that is the catch of a lifetime. Chub are greedy fish and will eat almost anything you can throw at them. I've had chub on artificial flies, boilies, bread, casters, cheese, chips, grasshoppers, luncheon meat, maggots, pellets, spinners, small fish, worms and even Polo mints! You can catch chub in an equally diverse number of ways. Trotting with a float is excellent. Alternatively, leger a bait close to sanctuary where the chub feel especially confident.

A beautiful chub lovingly returned to the water.

Bream

Bream are also a favourite species, especially with match anglers trying to build up a big weight of fish. A 5lb (2.2kg) bream is a good catch and a 10lb (4.4kg) fish is a specimen. You'll find bream in both stillwaters and slower-running rivers where they tend to avoid very fast water, but that's not always the case. Best bream bait includes bread, maggots and worms. Most bream are usually caught on the bottom using either a feeder or a straight leger weight. However, you can also catch them on wagglers up to a range of about 100–130ft (30–40m) in stillwaters.

Rudd

The rudd is exceptionally beautiful. Those golden scales and scarlet fins make it a favourite with every angler. Generally, rudd come from larger stillwaters. A 2lb (1kg) rudd is a specimen. Rudd take all the usual baits, but their favourites are artificial flies, bread and maggots. You can catch them on the bottom, but you can also find them on the surface and in midwater. Float fishing is an excellent way to catch these fish, but they will also sip in pieces of floating bread. Rudd are very skittish and the shoals are easily scared, so be prepared to fish mobile methods.

Perch

Another favourite is the heavily striped perch, which may also be recognised by its spiked dorsal fin. These fish are common in all European waters and weigh 5lb (2.2kg) or more. Catch a 2lb (1.4kg) fish, though and you've done well. You'll find perch in every type of still and running water, providing there is food present in the shape of small fish. Top baits for perch include maggots, worms, small dead fish and small artificial lures. They are particularly fond of tiny spinners. You can float fish, fish leger weights or feeders for perch, especially at distance, where you'll often find them in deeper lakes.

Dace

Dace is widespread throughout Europe. This fish looks very much like the chub but is smaller, slimmer and more silvery. As a result, it used to be called the dart in places. The dace is very much a fish which favours quick, clear, uncontaminated running waters. A 1lb (0.4kg) fish is the catch of a lifetime. The best baits for dace are maggots and tiny red worms. The best way to fish for them is trotting a stick float down a glide of water between 3 and 5ft (1 and 1.5m) deep. Dace are quick biters, so prepare for the float simply to vanish.

Charlie looks delighted with this fine bream.

The rudd is one of the most beautiful freshwater species.

A fine 2lb (1kg) perch in profile.

Crucian Carp

Crucian carp are found in pockets throughout Europe. Wherever these fish exist, they are very popular. Crucian carp do not grow as big as normal carp and a 2lb (1.4kg) fish is a specimen. These fish are magnificent, rather like small plates of gold. Crucian carp are nearly always found in stillwaters and they're timid biters. Best baits are maggots or very soft pieces of bread flake. Float fishing is by far the best way of picking up on their gentle bites.

Zander

Zander are predatory fish popular across Europe. They range in size between perch and pike – a 10lb (4.5kg) fish is good, while a 15lb (6.8kg) specimen is a real catch. Zander are found in both stillwaters and rivers and tend to hunt in packs, particularly at dusk through till dawn. Small dead baits are excellent for Zander, especially if they're given a bit of life. You'll also pick them up on artificial lures of most kinds. They're cunning fish, however, so you've got to work the artificials with great skill.

Asp

Asp are present in several parts of Europe. These are primarily – but not always – river fish. They look a little bit like chub, but they are more aggressive and predatory. They also grow a little bigger – I have seen asp in excess of 10lb (4.5kg). While you can catch asp on all normal baits, the best way to tackle them is with artificial lures, especially spinners. They will also take small dead baits, particularly if they are twitched to give them a little bit of life.

Eels

Finally, there are those strange anglers who like catching eels. Seriously, a big eel is a fascinating foe. You'll find them in both still and running water and in brackish lagoons around the coast. A 5lb (2.2kg) eel is considered to be a specimen, but they often grow to double this size. The best baits for eels are probably worms, followed by small fish, almost always fished on the bottom or just off it. Eels are very much creatures of the night and most serious eel anglers begin at dusk and fish through till dawn.

COARSE FISHING WATERS

Before I get onto the waters themselves, I'd like to have a quick look at one other all-important factor — the weather. The weather has a vital impact on both the water and the fish and so it is essential to give it some consideration. People have air-conditioning, central heating, clothing and all sorts of devices to make life much easier and more comfortable. Obviously fish don't have these luxuries. The entire life of a fish is spent looking for food, searching for a secure spot and trying to make itself as comfortable as possible whilst the conditions change around it.

There are some important considerations regarding the weather and its impact on coarse fishing waters. First, most fish species will either stop feeding or begin to look for shade if it's exceedingly hot. At times of very hot weather, you're probably best fishing at dusk and dawn to avoid the extreme heat of the midday sun. If you have to fish during the hottest part of the day, look for areas in which fish can shelter from direct sunlight.

Equally, you might find that fish feed best in the early afternoon if it's cold, since the light and warmth are both at their peak. Dusk is a good time too. Look for deep water where it's likely to be warmer.

The approach of high pressure is almost always good for nearly all fish species. If the pressure is settled and stable for long periods that also helps feeding confidence. Falling pressure is the worst. Fish especially don't like the initial period when the barometer is falling, but after a few days they will start to feed again.

Wind is an essential factor, notably on stillwaters. For example, most carp anglers like to fish into the wind because the oxygen is at its greatest and a lot of food is accumulated. As a result, the carp know there will be rich pickings. The wind also stirs up the bottom in shallow water and gives the swim a

Barbel, chub and roach will feed heavily in the slightly coloured water of this river.

slight colouring. This lulls the carp's wariness and also helps disguise your end tackle.

Rain is also an important element, especially in the river environment. The more it rains, the more a river rises and the more colour thickens up. A rising, colouring river is generally excellent. You'll also find that wary fish feed better in coloured water than clear water – that's why big catches of barbel and chub are caught at this time. As the water begins to fall and the colour drains out of it, the fishing will gradually slow down. When the river is clear again, you'll find you have problems during the daytime using anything but light tackle and small baits.

UNDERSTANDING RIVERS

If you're going to catch fish, it's essential that you learn to read rivers and have the confidence in your decisions. All rivers have elements in common and it's important to look for these in order to locate the fish and decide where you're going to settle.

One of the most important considerations on any river is the current itself. All rivers flow at different speeds toward the sea. Certain fish prefer faster currents; others slower ones. It's important to know what type of current the fish that you're after like, because that's where you'll find them. For example, barbel prefer quick water and you'll find them where the water moves fast over stony bottoms. Bream prefer the slower, deeper water of a river. Chub are happy everywhere. Dace prefer shallow water with a quick push of current. Pike often hang in the deep slacks but then venture out in the current to hunt for food.

Remember that a quick current is generally more difficult to fish than a slow one. You'll have to learn to mend the line, which means keeping it straight to the float or the lead without a big loop forming as the current pushes it downstream. Sometimes, it's best to fish slower water until you become more confident with rivers. A slower current allows you to present your bait in a much more relaxed fashion.

Always keep your eyes open for weirs and mill pools. These always attract fish, in part because of

A favourite mill pool on a lowland river. Big bream, chub and barbel can be found in the oxygenated, food-rich stream.

A big push of quick-moving water. In the winter, chub can be found in runs such as this one.

The river just upstream of a mill is a good place to locate shoals of roach. They also love extensive reed beds and overhanging willows.

the oxygen that is forced into the water by the flow through the mill gates. Generally, there is also a good depth to mill pools and fish like depth for security. The bottom of mill pools is nearly always heavily covered in rocks, masonry and rubbish thrown in over the generations. All these harbour extensive food stocks, which again hold fish for long periods.

Nearly all rivers are made up of a series of deep pools and shallower, faster, stony rapids. Fish will often use these rapids to feed and then move into the pools either upstream or downstream to rest. As a rough guide, you're probably better fishing the rapids early and late in the day when the fish are actively feeding. Attack the deeper pools during the heat of the day when the fish are more lethargic.

Look for features in and alongside the river that may offer protection and food. Overhanging and fallen trees are a perfect example. Chub love to

However small, weir pools always attract fish. Notice the oxygen being pumped in by the falling water.

This angler is fishing the crease — the seam of water between a fast current and a slow, deep slack. Fish move in and out of the two zones since food tends to congregate here.

hide under dense tree growth — birds cannot attack them from above and a lot of insect food falls from the branches. You'll also find that the light is less intense under trees. This is important in bright sunlight, which most fish avoid.

Bridges provide shelter from the sunlight and also generate food. Over the years, brickwork falls in to create features on the bottom where insects congregate. The current is quick through the arches of bridges and this carries a lot of food to the fish waiting in the pool beneath. If you dive a pool beneath a bridge, you'll find all sorts of rubbish there — anything from old bits of cars to shopping carts. All these things provide shelter for the fish and shelter for the insects on which they feed.

Bridges are frequent top features on rivers.

Unless they have been butchered by dredging and bad river management, most rivers naturally form a series of bends as they wind their way across the flood plain. These bends are extremely important. The current tends to be slower on the inside of a bend and a lot of food falls to the bottom. This attracts a lot of fish. Generally, there is also deeper water on the inside of most river bends, which species such as barbel, bream and chub favour.

River bends are also essential when the water is high. Floods tend to push shoals of fish out of their normal swims. A bend provides protection and by slowing the river down, allows fish to rest there.

You can never ignore artificial structures. Jetties and fishing platforms are magnets for all sorts of fish. Many species love rocks and old wooden pilings for shelter and protection. Again, insects tend to congregate on these structures, providing plenty of food for the fish. Some of the best barbel I've ever seen were living in the sunken shell of an old boat. On another occasion, the rotting carcass of a drowned cow notably attracted a shoal of chub, which took refuge inside the ribcage!

Above all, never be apprehensive if you're fishing a big river. Look carefully at the watercourse and break it down into small sections. Look for notable characteristics. Study any signs that tell you something is different. Learn to appreciate what the current is doing. Just relax, regard the river as a friend and you're well on the way to success.

River bends are always worth investigating. Food tends to accumulate in the slower, deeper water.

READING STILLWATERS

Don't be frightened by big stillwaters and think they are unreadable – if you take your time, all will become clear and you'll be able to read even vast reservoirs.

Do not fish at the first likely place that you come to. Take time to walk round any stillwaters, preferably with Polaroid glasses and even a pair of binoculars. Look for actively feeding fish. You'll often see areas of water stained by mud. This has been uprooted by bream and carp as they burrow in the bottom silt. Look out diving birds, such as grebes, because they will tell you about the location of small fish. Find those and you've often located bigger predators. Look for fish crashing out or rolling on the surface. If the water is rippled, look for the appearance of flat areas, often the size of a table top. These are created by fish turning underneath the water's surface, intercepting food items as they rise to the surface. Always look closely at the windward shore of any stillwaters. This is where there is likely to be more colour, more oxygen and more food washed up.

Dams and other areas of deep water are a good place to consider. In the summer, fish will retreat to deeper water to escape the bright light and heat. It's the same in the winter, when the temperatures plummet. The deepest water will be the most comfortable for all coarse species.

Take time out to explore stillwaters before making a choice on swim. If you can see the fish you're well on the way to success.

A winter weir pool is often home to chub, barbel, roach and dace.

be easy to fish into weed but if that's where they are, you've got to make the effort.

There are lots of other features that make your stillwaters readable. For example, feeder streams are highly sought after by the fish. These bring in cool water in the summer months, which fish find extremely attractive. Feeder streams also wash in a great deal of food. Islands are a key feature of many stillwaters. Fish love the protection offered by the margins of the island so they can avoid predators such as cormorants and otters. Caterpillars and flies also drop from the branches of island trees and fish learn to look for these items, especially when a brisk wind is blowing.

It always pays to look at the shallows, too. It is here that fish will spend a lot of their time feeding, because insect populations in shallow water are particularly rich. Often you'll see fish muddying the bottom or, if the water is really shallow, you might see their tails emerge as they feed head down over the bed.

Most shallows are surrounded by reeds and rushes. Fish, especially carp, prefer to feed in the middle of these reed beds and you'll often see the reeds shaking as the fish muscle in and burrow in the mud. The shallows are particularly worth fishing at dawn and again at dusk, because fish will drift to deeper water for security during the heat and brightness of the day.

All types of vegetation are important to fish. Vegetation offers shelter from predators, harbours a lot of food and at certain times of the year, also provides structure around which to spawn. Favourite types of vegetation include lily beds, which shelter fish from the sun and harbour a lot of food on their stems. More fish will be in weed than outside it. It might not always

Vegetation is an important aid to find fish. Floating lily pads are always a sure sign.

Any areas of riverbank with heavy tree growth are worth investigating. Over the years, the leaves fall into the water and a rich silt builds up

Never neglect banksides shrouded by trees.

on the riverbed. You'll often find extensive beds of bloodworms in this nutrient-rich environment. The tiny red wormlike insects are favourite food of species such as bream, carp and tench.

It's important to identify the bottom contours of any lake. Sometimes you'll be able to see where the shallows extend and where they drop off into deeper, darker water using Polaroids. Fish like to patrol the ledges between the shallows and deeper water and they are important angling ambush points for bream, carp, roach and tench. In artificial lakes, you'll frequently find a deep, central channel that runs from a feeder stream down toward the dam. This deeper water is always a magnet during the heat of the midday sun.

Look for any "unique selling points" on your stillwaters. A jetty can be attractive to perch that love to rub their flanks on rotting bits of woodwork

and crumbling masonry. The darkness of an old boathouse often attracts roach and rudd during the heat of the day. Perch like to shelter underneath moored boats. In reservoirs, the remains of flooded buildings and walls are always worth investigating. Remember that fish aren't scattered randomly round any stillwaters like the currants in a fruitcake. If you understand what the fish want – food, security and comfort – you're well on the way to reading your stillwaters, no matter how large and intimidating it might seem at first sight.

A bridge holds back the force of the river, leading to a deep, slow swim much favoured by roach and bream. Always search out unusual spots like this.

COARSE FISHING TACKLE

Good tackle is essential. If it's good quality you'll find it easier to use and more reliable. And if you do hook a big fish, it's good to have confidence in the tackle in your hand. Don't be afraid of the tackle shop. Sometimes there is just so much for

Buy the best rods you can afford. Good materials, design and workmanship are invaluable.

sale that it can look baffling and intimidating. Take your time, only buy what you need and ask for good advice. These are the essential items of tackle you're going to need.

Rods

I could just about do all my coarse fishing with three types of rod. One of them would be what in Britain is called an Avon-style rod. It would be round 11ft (3.4m) long with a nice steady "through" action, which means it bends nicely from the handle right through to the tip when under pressure. It will have a test curve of around 1.5lb (0.7kg). This simply means that a weight of 1.5lb (0.7kg) will bend the rod into a quarter circle. With this type of rod I'd be able to fish most sorts of baits for most sorts of species, especially with legers and feeders. I might want an attachment on the top ring so that I could screw in a quiver tip if extra sensitivity were needed. A quiver

tip is simply a little bit finer than the normal rod tip and shows up bites better. I'd also be able to fish for carp up to 20lb (9kg) with this rod and for fish on the surface with floating crust – chub or carp again, for example. I'd also be able to fish smaller

A "professional" carp set up. Notice the three matched rods and reels, the electronic bite indicators and the precision of the set up.

artificials, for pike up to 20lb (9kg) and for asp, perch and Zander. For 70 percent of my fishing, I wouldn't need to look at another rod.

I'd also choose a float rod of about 13 ft (3.9m) in length. I love float fishing on both rivers and stillwaters and sometimes you need that extra 2ft (0.6m) in length to give you extra control. The rod will probably have a test curve of just under 1lb (0.4kg) and again, it will have a nice "through" action to it to cushion the lunges of big fish.

Finally, I'd choose a rod of 11.5ft (3.5m) in length with a test curve of around 2–2.25lb (0.9–1kg). I would use this for heavier carp fishing, for dead baiting for pike and for heavier spinning with bigger lures than the Avon rod can cope with.

Go into any tackle shop and you'll see armouries of rods. Some are long, some are short, some are heavy and some are light, but these three are the ideal ones to start with. With them in your possession, there's hardly any coarse fishing situation that's going to catch you out.

Reels

There are three major types of reels for the coarse fisherman: multipliers, centrepins and fixed spool reels. However, for 99 percent of your coarse fishing, a fixed spool reel is all you're going to need. These are the easiest reels to use and modern models are generally of fabulous quality. The reels all have a clutch so you can set the spool to give under tension. Don't tighten up too much or the spool won't be able to rotate and give line to a running fish. One medium-sized fixed spool reel will probably do for the vast majority of your coarse fishing – at least to begin with. As you build up, I would recommend a light fixed spool, a medium-sized fixed spool and a heavier fixed spool for carp and pike fishing.

You'll need separate spools to take different line strengths to suit the different styles of fishing, the different water types and the different fish species that you're pursuing.

This fine tench was caught on a Centre pin reel rather than a fixed spool. Centre pins are especially useful on rivers when fishing close in on stillwaters.

Two rods and fixed spool reels mounted on rod rests. Notice that electronic bite indicators are used. Hangers swing beneath the rod and jerk upward when a bite is registered.

This angler uses the touch legering technique on a fixed spool reel.

The line flies off a fixed spool reel as the bait is cast.

For roach and perch, fish a waggler like this in stillwaters close to the rushes.

Lines

I would suggest that you always have a range of spools to hand that hold different breaking strain lines. At the lightest, I would go for a spool with 3lb (1.4kg) breaking strain. This is perfect for species such as dace, roach and rudd. Then I would recommend a spool of 5lb (2.3kg) breaking strain line. This will cope with chub and tench. For example, a spool with 8lb (3.6kg) line is probably going to be perfect for smaller carp, asp and particularly, for barbel. If you're ambitious, you should also have a spool of around 12lb (5.5kg) line for larger carp and bigger pike. Always buy top-quality line. If it's cheap, it will break, degrade and tangle easily.

Floats

Of course, you can fish for most coarse species on the bottom, but you'll need to float fish, too, to get the very best out of the sport. For stillwaters, you need a selection of wagglers, which are fixed onto the line by their bottom end only. I would recommend you buy a selection of weighted and non-weighted wagglers. The weighted ones cock by themselves. You'll need wagglers in small, medium and large sizes to cope with different conditions and allow you to cast further distances.

There's a wide variety of river floats. You'll need some stick floats for sensitive, precision fishing at shorter range. Avon floats have bigger, more bulbous tops to them and are better for use with big baits in faster currents. You can use these to trot bread flake, luncheon meat and worms for long distances. There are endless other varieties of floats, but don't be confused. Start off with these three first and you'll find that they will be fine for 95 percent of your coarse fishing situations.

A fine chub caught on a combination of block-end feeder and maggot.

A typical river float was used to catch this fine roach.

Leads and feeders

Leads are put on the line to take the bait down to the bottom of the water column and anchor it there. Sometimes, you might want to use a round lead that rolls a little bit in the current and moves the bait to search fish out. A totally flat lead is the best way to anchor a bait completely. Choose a variety of different lead shapes and weights to suit every situation that you're likely to face. Of course, remember the heavier the current, the bigger the lead you're going to need.

Swim feeders do much the same job as a lead. However, they also carry free items of food to the fish to encourage them to feed on the hook bait. Cage feeders are useful for packing with ground bait and loose hook bait samples. A closed feeder is perfect for filling with maggots that will slowly wriggle out through the holes during the course of the cast.

A common technique in modern coarse fishing is the use of a method feeder. This is packed with ground bait and hook bait samples and the hook is actually buried into the mix. The fish comes along, browses on the great pile of ground bait, comes across the hook bait and virtually hooks itself.

Again, stock with caged, closed and method feeders and buy a couple of each in several sizes.

Hooks

There's nothing more important than your hook and it's essential to buy hooks in a variety of sizes. The biggest I would choose are size 2 for big carp and big baits such as large pieces of bread. I would then buy a packet of hooks in each and every size up to around size 20, which is the smallest I would recommend for most fishing. The smaller hooks, in sizes 16, 18 and 20, are perfect for tiny baits such as casters and maggots. Medium-sized hooks, such as 10 and 12 are good for bread flake and sweetcorn. Always try to match the hook size to the bait. For example, a lobworm sits nicely on a size 8 or 10.

I tend to fish increasingly with barbless hooks. These are much easier on the fish and your own finger if disaster strikes. Microbarbs are available in many brands if you don't want to go entirely barbless. An alternative is to buy a barbed hook and crush down the barb with forceps.

Most of my hooks are eye hooks and I tie them to the line using a blood knot, although there are many other different knot types. For me, the blood knot is simple and effective and has never let me down.

When it comes to pike fishing, especially using dead baits, it's common to use treble hooks. These hooks can be extremely difficult to remove from the pike's mouth, especially if the bait is lodged deep down in the fish's throat. For this reason, I use large single hooks for my pike fishing as well as my general coarse fishing.

Accessories

You're probably going to need a bag in which to carry all your kit. You'll probably also need a rod rest to put your rod on when you're not actually holding it. Electronic bite indicators are also useful for alerting you to a run, especially if you are carp fishing fishing long sessions for bream and tench. A landing net is essential, too. Without a landing net you just can't get that better fish out onto the bank. I deplore holding fish in keep nets, but occasionally it's useful to have a soft sack in which

The typical set up for tench or bream: two rods on electronic bite indicators with hangers beneath.

to hold a fish while it recovers from the exertion of a fight. Forceps are also very important. With your forceps, you can flatten down the barb on a hook and more importantly, slip the hook out of a hooked fish.

Importantly, you'll also need a tin or two of shot. These come in an assortment of sizes and they are used to put on the line to cock a float. You'll also need bait boxes, particularly for maggots, sweetcorn and worms. A small bucket is extremely useful for mixing ground bait.

A landing net is absolutely essential for bigger fish.

It's essential that your clothing is up to the job. If you're cold and wet or hot and sticky then you won't enjoy the fishing experience. If you're not comfortable, you'll lose concentration and you won't fish to your best potential. Most clothing these days is layered. You have a warm inner layer, mostly of artificial fibres. This will be tight-fitting and will trap a layer of warm air from your body. You'll then have a mid-layer of artificial fleece. This will prevent any heat escaping from your body and will also shield you from cold air. A waterproof top layer is worn over the entire clothing system. This should be windproof as well as waterproof, but it should also be breathable so that your own perspiration can wick away into the atmosphere.

In cold weather, you'll also need a hat. A warm beanie is perfect if it's not too wet. If you're fishing in driving rain or snow, a waterproof hood will also be necessary. Gloves and thermal socks complete your armoury against cold weather.

Below-zero conditions demand the very best clothing to keep warm.

In warm weather, make sure all your exposed areas of skin are covered from the sun or protected by a high-factor sunscreen or sunblock. There's an increased risk of sunburn, not only from direct sunlight, but also from the sun's reflection on the

Father and son fish for barbel in the middle of the river.

water. Don't fish for too long in very bright sunlight. Look for shady spots. If you have to fish in the open, do so for short periods and then retire to the shade to recover. Take plenty of liquids with you and constantly rehydrate.

Polaroid glasses are an essential item of any coarse angler's tackle. For a start, they protect your eyes from the glare of strong sunlight. Second, they shield your eyes against any accidental miscast that could potentially damage your eyesight. Polaroids are also an invaluable aid to your fishing success, because they allow you to see the fish feeding beneath the surface glare of the water. With Polaroids, you can see what the fish are doing and how they are feeding in a way that is impossible without them.

You'll need to think carefully about your footwear. Unless it's warm, you'll need something waterproof on your feet. I almost always wear breathable chestwaders when I'm fishing. When it's wet, the chestwaders keep me totally dry. When it's cold, they keep out the wind. If I want to wade in the margins of a river or stillwaters, I can, providing I'm sure it is safe to do so. I choose boots with a good grip so there is little danger of slipping down a steep bank.

You can buy neoprene chestwaders to keep warm in the winter but they are difficult to walk in comfortably for great distances. Wellingtons are cheaper, but they are not as adaptable as waders.

Chestwaders are great for getting out into the river. Even on hot days, you can walk long distances if the chestwaders are breathable.

COARSE FISHING BAIT

The whole essence of coarse fishing is that of fishing with a bait to entice a fish into making a mistake. Bait choice is key to what we do and it must always be of the highest quality.

Traditional baits

Traditional baits have been around for decades and have really proved their worth. Top of the list must be bread. You can simply pull pieces of bread and press them onto the shank of the hook. This is called bread flake. Alternatively, you can wet the bread with water and mold it into a paste that can then be enhanced with colourings and flavourings. If you grate in a little cheese, this will give it a really good texture and strong taste. The crust of a loaf is also useful. You can fish little pieces anchored to the bottom with a lead or use larger pieces floating on the surface for carp and chub.

A piece of bread flake squeezed onto the hook is one of the oldest and most successful baits for bream, carp, roach and tench.

A piece of floating crust on a size 2 or 4 hook is perfect bait for a carp on a hot day when the fish swim close to the surface.

Luncheon meat is one of the oldest and most successful baits for chub and barbel. Simply pull the luncheon meat out of the tin and put it on the hook quite ragged. Bits of meat fall away to attract fish.

Particle bait comes in many varieties. It's best to get them properly prepared like this to avoid endangering the health of the fish.

Another traditional bait is the ever popular luncheon meat – in all its various forms. Buy the best for good taste and a firm texture. Meatballs are also excellent for barbel and chub.

Sweetcorn has become a hugely popular bait among anglers over the last 30 years. It's easy to buy, easy to prepare and easy to use. Most species of fish absolutely adore sweetcorn. Try also coloured grains of sweetcorn if fish have wised up to the normal yellow variety. Red is excellent.

Particle baits

Particle bait is the term used for small baits used in large quantities. The most common particle bait is the maggot. All fish species adore maggots and you can loose-feed maggots around your float or put them in a feeder if you're fishing at distance on the bottom. My favourite two colours are white and red, but some people swear by brown or even green! When maggots begin to transform into flies, they become

casters. These are particularly attractive to fish such as bream, roach and tench, but the cases are brittle and break off easily.

Hempseed is especially good for pulling in carp, tench, bream and barbel, driving them into a feeding frenzy.

A well-stocked shelf of boilies. Buy them vacuum-packed and they will stay fresh for a long time.

Many boilies are sold frozen. They can be stored in the freezer almost indefinitely, waiting to be used on a long session.

Boiled hemp seed is irresistible to most members of the carp family and especially barbel, roach and tench. The problem is that it's easy to get fish preoccupied with feeding on the hemp to the point that they refuse a slightly larger hook bait. It's often a good idea to fish a mix of hemp, casters and maggots. You can put casters or maggots on the hook more easily than the hemp and they give the fish a larger bait to home in on.

Modern baits — boilies and pellets

Boilies first began to appear in the 1970s and the 1980s. The concept is that they are attractive to carp in particular, but also because they have a hard-boiled outer shell. As a result, they can't be picked to bits by smaller, "nuisance" species such as roach. One appeal of the boily is that they can be made in many different sizes, with many different colours and with many different flavourings. Boilies are made from a concoction of different powders, different colourings and different flavourings and are generally mixed together with milk and/or eggs. Unless you're a truly dedicated carp angler, however,

it's probably best to buy ready-made boilies from the tackle shop. These are vacuum packed and will last for ages. It's a good idea to ask advice before you splash out a lot of money on boilies. Certain carp waters have certain preferences, so it's good to go for a range that you know has a track record. Think about the size of boily, too. If the lake has a lot of big roach in it, for example, smaller-diameter boilies will be picked off by them and you'll have to go larger — even up to 0.8in (2cm) to avoid them.

Pellets are relative newcomers to the bait scene. The most popular are halibut pellets, but they are available in a number of flavours. Smaller pellets of 0.15–0.23in (4–6mm) are useful as loose feed to attract fish such as barbel, bream, carp, chub, roach and tench into the swim. You can then use larger pellets — 0.3, 0.39 or 0.46in (8, 10 or 12mm) — on the hook. Generally, these are too hard to thread onto the hook directly and they're often held in place by what we call the bait band. Alternatively, you can buy drilled pellets and place them on a hair rig.

You can buy many types of commercial ground baits. Different ground baits attract different fish species so take time to read the packets carefully.

Small mackerel make a perfect dead bait. They're tough, streamlined and can be cast long distances.

Ground baits

Ground bait is extremely useful to attract fish into the swim. Most ground bait should break up on impact with the surface of the water and then disperse as a colourful cloud to create the impression of food falling from above. It's a good idea to work different food items into the basic ground bait mix to keep fish interested. Casters and maggots are perfect for this purpose. Try hempseed, sweetcorn and small pellets, too.

If you're fishing at range, try to keep the ground bait dry and form it into hard-pressed balls. Use a catapult to fire them out long distances. With experience, your accuracy will improve. You can also use ground bait to pack into cage feeders. When the cage feeder settles on the bottom, the ground bait slowly swells, explodes and forms a carpet around the hook bait.

There are all manner of different types of ground bait for sale in most tackle shops. The choice is bewildering, but I always like anything that contains ground hempseed.

Dead baits

Dead baits are an essential part of the predator angler's armoury. Pike in particular, but also perch and Zander, will take dead baits of all types. Generally, dead baits fall into two categories: freshwater or sea baits. Favourite freshwater baits include small bream, dace, perch, roach and sections of eel. It's important for the conservation of fish stocks to ensure that these baits are not netted from wild fisheries, where the future of the fish is not assured.

The best sea baits include herring, mackerel, smelt, sprat and all sorts of exotics such as sea lamprey and different kinds of snapper.

If you've got large dead baits, it pays to cut them into smaller sections. I prefer tail sections, but a lot of fish have been caught on the head alone. Experiment with different types of dead bait. One day, you'll find that pike only take sardines, but the next day they're only interested in roach. Predators are capricious and if you're going to have constant success then it's good to ring every possible variation.

Keep your baits frozen in a dedicated freezer. That way you'll always have them ready at short notice for any fishing expedition.

Artificial lures

Every predator angler should have an armoury of metal, plastic, rubber and wood lures, which are made to imitate dying or wounded smaller fish. The whole importance behind lure fishing is to make this artificial creation look as real as possible and excite the predator's hunger and interest.

Spinners have been extremely popular for centuries. These lures feature a blade that revolves in the water and flashes as you retrieve the spinner toward the bank. Sometimes the addition of a bit of red wool on the treble hook at the rear provokes a serious attack.

Spoons have been equally successful. As their name suggests, these are pieces of metal – mostly silver or bronze – that are hammered in the shape of a spool so that they wobble their way through the water when retrieved. These are particularly useful for big waters and suspicious pike.

Plugs can be made of a variety of materials and they are fashioned to look like real fish. Sometimes they are made of wood and other times plastic or metal. Some plugs are designed to work on the surface with a chugging, splashing motion. Other plugs work midwater – between 3.2 and 6.4ft (1 and 2m) in depth – while other plugs are created to fish way beneath that. Deep-water plugs can be retrieved at depths in excess of 32ft (10m) and are extremely useful for large, deep reservoirs.

My favourites are lures made out of rubber – the famous rubber fish. Retrieved through the water, these look fantastic. You can buy them in a variety of shapes and colours – all with different actions. One great thing about rubbers is that when a pike holds

A very successful plastic lure. The slits in the body allow the tail section to work with real power. Notice there is only one set of trebles on this lure. There is also a big snap link at the head of the lure. You don't want flimsy lures when you're after big fish.

One of my favourite plugs. This works close to the surface with a quick, twisting motion. Pike love it.

Probably my favourite lure — a beautifully coloured and beautifully designed rubber fish. The large tail works perfectly and the rubber texture makes the bait feel exactly like a real fish. The single hook makes for an easy release of the predator.

them, the feel is similar to a real fish. By comparison, a plug is brittle and hard. Another advantage with rubbers is that they often come equipped with a single, large hook. This makes unhooking much easier.

Remember that all these lures (and dead baits) have to be fished with a wire trace — the sharp teeth of a pike will sever a nylon line. Try to keep your lures systematically in a purpose-built bag. If they all get jumbled together, you'll find they come out in huge tangles. Look after the treble hooks on the lures. It's a good idea to press the barbs down with your forceps — both for the fish's sake and your own to prevent an accident. You can also buy plastic "hoods" that slip on treble hooks to prevent them from tangling and becoming a danger as you fumble in the tackle bag.

Always keep your lures in a warm, dry place so they don't corrode and rust. They can be expensive, so it makes sense to look after them.

This is a novel way to transport your lures during a daylong session. Make sure they don't tangle so you can get at them easily. The more times you experiment with a lure, the more success you will have.

COARSE FISHING SKILLS
AND TECHNIQUES

Casting

Getting your bait and tackle in the water exactly where you want it is a basic skill. Accurate casting, especially at range, is an art. Let's look at some of the main considerations in successful casting. Very often, it's vital that your bait and terminal gear — either a float, lead or feeder — enters the water quite softly. To ensure soft entry, you need to slow down the rate that the tackle is flying through the air just before it enters the water. The method to use is known as "feathering". You need to dab you finger on the spool of the reel as the float or lead nears its destination. This slows down the rate at which the float or lead enters the water and the splash is therefore much reduced. It's an essential skill to learn in shallow water, particularly when fishing for shy species such as bream or carp.

Look carefully around you before casting. Be aware of any potential snags or hazards. Overhanging trees are an obvious danger, but watch for beds of weed, rush and low bridges or fences behind you.

In a margin of heavy reeds, you may need to tread out into clearer water if you're going to cast long distances and work your lure effectively.

Lee is ready to launch carp bait a long way out into the lake. Notice how the rod is suspended over his head and how he is still for a moment to allow everything to settle before the cast.

It's extremely important to take your time when casting. Make sure that you're poised and in control. It's best if your float or lead hangs about 3–4.5ft (0.9–1.4m) beneath your rod tip as you look back at it over your casting shoulder. Let it steady itself before casting out. The more you try to rush things, the more tangles will ensue.

It's also important to watch out for gusts of wind that will pull your tackle off its intended course through the air toward the water. Allow for a little movement with the breeze. If the wind is blowing left to right, for example, then aim into the wind a little to drop the gear exactly where you want it. Practice really does make perfect and sometimes the initial cast will be trial and error.

You cannot cast successfully unless your equipment is up to the job. Your rod is an essential piece of kit. If you're casting a float, a road that's too short won't have the necessary leverage to cast either at distance or with any degree of accuracy. Your reel, too, is absolutely essential. Make sure that the spool is full nearly to the rim to allow the line to fly off more easily and with greater control. Check for any knots close to the surface of the line on your spool. These will catch as the loops of line fly over it. Try not to cast too light a float if you want to achieve distance or you're fishing into a heavy wind. It's always better to go heavier and maintain control. Remember, too, that the finer diameter of your line, the further you're likely to be able to cast. Heavier line means reduced distance because of the increased friction of the line through the rings.

Out it goes. Ian demonstrates perfect technique to putting bait out at around 239 ft (73m).

A surface lure is cast out into the water from under a mass of overhanging trees. The lure is retrieved and shape looms behind it. A hit. A strike. A fish on.

Timing is critical when casting. It's obvious to relax, take your time and remain in control. Keep practising the technique until you know when to raise your finger from the spool and let the line fly out. If you take your finger off the spool too quickly, the cast will flop behind you. If you remove your finger too late, the cast will splash clumsily in the water right in front of you. Eventually, timing will become second nature and you'll do it perfectly each and every time.

Soon you'll learn that there are different types of cast. Sometimes an underhand cast is used to flick

A fine carp comes to the net. It's good when it comes right.

your gear out under some overhanging trees or a low bridge. Casting sideways allows you to flick your bait just around the lip of a bed of weeds. Most of these casts are trying to achieve relatively short ranges. Long-range casting is an entirely new ball game.

It is absolutely essential to master the techniques of long casting, especially in carp fishing. That's why long, powerful rods allied with heavy leads and tangleproof rigs have become fashionable. However, you can also cast long distances with an 11ft (3.4m) rod and a heavily loaded feeder. The cast to use is the overhead. Poise the bait behind your back. Your left hand holds the rod down toward the base of the handle. Your right hand is over the reel with your finger controlling the line. Aim to make the cast a smooth, pendulum-like motion but constantly accelerating with ever-increasing speed. Don't cast at the horizon first off. Start with moderate distances of 65–98ft (20–30m) and build up from there. Remember that the more effort you put into the cast, the more likely you are to lose accuracy and tangle the line.

Casting is an art form that is relatively easy to learn and improves with practise. Simply follow the basic rules and accuracy and distance will both improve very quickly. Be patient.

THE ULTIMATE GUIDE TO FISHING

A float on the stream — the art of coarse fishing.

Striking

So, you've cast out successfully and registered a bite. It's amazing how many of those bites are lost because of basic mistakes. Firstly, you've got to get your timing right. It's all too easy to hurry the strike and pull the bait out of the fish's mouth. Generally, it's best to strike more slowly and give the fish time to catch the bait. This is especially true if you're using big bait, when it often pays to wait until you see the line draw tight. Of course, some fish, such as the dace, bite with lightning speed. If you don't hit these fish instantly, you'll miss them. As a general rule, however, try not to strike too soon. Curb your enthusiasm and be patient.

However, you shouldn't delay a strike too long or one of two things might happen. First, the fish might feel resistance and drop the bait and then you'll miss your chance. Alternatively, the fish might engulf the bait and swallow it, obviously suffering when it comes to unhooking. Once again, the real answer lies with experimentation and experience. Trust your gut instinct, too. Frequently, you'll know instinctively when the time is right to set the hook.

Make your strike a good one. Most fish are lost through soft strikes rather than striking too powerfully.

The power of the strike is also very important. You'll pull the fish through the water if you strike too powerfully and it will end up somewhere in the undergrowth behind you. Another problem when you strike too hard, especially with big fish, is that you run the real risk of breaking your line. For this reason, I always set the clutch of my reel so the line is relatively slack and will give a bit in an emergency. To set the clutch on the reel, I like to hold the line a few inches away from the reel, give it a pull and hear that check whine without too much effort.

However, striking too softly is just as ineffective as striking too hard. It takes force to set the hook into a fish, especially at distance. If you're fishing at distances more than 65ft (20m), for example, then it pays to keep the strike going right over your shoulder until you feel the fish. If you stop the strike too abruptly, you might not pick up enough line to sink the hook into the fish. Often you think the fish is off but, suddenly, you feel that satisfying clunk and you know there's a hook up.

There are another couple of points to bear in mind. Make sure you're aware of any potential hazards. For example, you don't want to strike abruptly and end up with your rod tip stuck in branches above. Make sure your hook is sharp, too. Just draw it across the surface of your nail and see if it makes a scratch mark – it should if it is sharp enough. And remember that a barbless hook sinks into the flesh much more easily and painlessly than a barbed one.

Playing and landing

Fish on! An exciting moment. However, it's all too easy to make mistakes and be disappointed. Small fish are easily reeled in and swung to hand but anything over 1lb (0.4kg) requires different techniques. If you're stuck into something as big as 40lb (18kg), then you've really got to consider what you're doing. Let's look at the rules.

Is that a bite? Sometimes carp will tear off when they are hit by a self-hooking rig. Sometimes, they are more circumspect and the bite is tiny.

Keep cool and calm during the final stages of the battle. Above all, don't chase a fish with the landing net; try to guide the fish toward it instead.

Holding a big fish in a current, such as this, takes confidence in your gear and the experience to know how far you can push both rod and line.

The first rule is that the clutch on your reel shouldn't be set too tight or too slack. Ideally, it should give line under a moderate amount of pressure. Hold the line in your hand and pull the rod round. When the tip is at right angles, the clutch should be able to give line. If it gives line too soon, tighten it up. If it doesn't give any line, slacken it off until it does. Also remember that if you're fishing in a dangerous area with lots of sunken branches then you don't want your fish to run far. In these circumstances you might decide to tighten up the clutch considerably, barely any line is given at all. As always, consider the situation and come to a rational decision.

The second rule is to keep your rod as close to the vertical as possible. The whole concept of playing a good fish is that the rod acts as a cushion to the runs of the fish. If you point your rod toward the water then the spring of its action is negated. The fish is simply pulling on the line without any buffer and a breakage is almost inevitable.

There are certain techniques that are vital to master when you're playing big fish. The first one is pumping. It's almost impossible to land a real biggie without this skill, but the technique is easy to master. Simply lower your rod tip toward the water and pull the fish slowly toward you until the rod is almost vertical. Then lower the rod smoothly back to its original position, reeling in smoothly as you do so. Keep on repeating the process. Gradually, you'll move the fish smoothly up through the water and closer to you every time. If you sense that the fish isn't coming but preparing for another long, unstoppable run, then stop the pumping process and ensure the clutch can give line. You can restart the pumping process once the fish has run and has tired.

It's also important to be aware of side strain. If a big fish is running toward a reed bed on your left, for example, then push your rod out as far as possible across the water and pull it to the right. The idea is that you'll turn the fish's head and avert the danger. Always be aware of where the fish is and what it's running toward. If you see the fish heading toward some dangerous snags, then you have simply got to put your finger on the spool and stop giving the fish line. It's better to go for broke than end up with a fish in the snags. You'll be amazed at how much pressure you can put on a fish if your tackle is sound.

More fish are lost close to the bank than at any other time. Some species, such as the barbel, make one, if not two or three, surging runs just when you think you've finally got them conquered. It's a good idea to keep low on the skyline so that your silhouette doesn't alarm a fish unnecessarily. Make sure your clutch isn't too tight so that it can deal with any last-minute rushes. Also remember that you've got less line out close to the bank, so the elasticity of the rod and the line is much reduced. Put your landing net in the water gently without splash to avoid alarming the fish and causing another run. Bring the fish to the net rather than chase the fish with the net. If you splash your net after the fish then it will simply fight harder and a break will be inevitable. If you're fishing with a friend, ask him or her to do the netting until you're more confident. Once the fish is secure over the net then lift it quickly and smoothly.

If the fish is big, don't try to lift it out by the handle of the net. Simply push the handle through your hands and grab hold of the rim of the net. If the fish is really big, don't even lift it by the rim but hold the mesh itself.

Mike turns a big fish away from danger.

A big barbel has rolled and is running yet again. This is a critical moment. Too tight a clutch can spell disaster.

When a float is fished on stillwaters and tench are piling up the bubbles, this is a good indicator you're in the right zone close to feeding fish.

FLOAT FISHING ON STILLWATERS AND MOVING WATER

Why float fish at all? Firstly, the float provides an excellent indication of a fish taking the bait. Secondly, using a float you can suspend the bait at any depth – from just under the surface to the bottom. Fish are used to intercepting food in midwater. That's exactly where your bait will sit if you use a float. Thirdly and finally, you can use a float to take the bait to all those places you can't reach by casting directly, for example, under branches and bridges. On a river, the current takes your float and bait a long way, so you're constantly exploring new water and increasing your chances of finding fish.

First let's look at float fishing on stillwaters. The most commonly used float here is the waggler. You attach a waggler to the line by its bottom end only. The most common way of fixing the waggler on the line is by locking it in place with a couple of split

Karim is fishing the waggler float for tench just past his rod tip. This is an exercise in concentration.

Waggler fishing on stillwaters is a great way of presenting the bait accurately. Shot down the float just a little bit more so that less of the tip is showing at the surface of the water.

shot. Use soft split shot so you can move them up and down the line to increase or decrease the depth at which your bait is fishing without damaging the line in the process. When you're float fishing, you often want to experiment with different depths so this is extremely important.

The waggler is a long, slim float and perfect for stillwaters. It's delicate, sensitive and registers bites well. You can use a waggler to suspend the bait anywhere from just under the surface to the bottom of the water. One of my favourite techniques is to set up the waggler with bait just over half depth, generally using maggots. Then I'll use a catapult to shoot maggots around the float and pull the fish in. Soon, they'll come across your hook bait and the waggler will dive.

The two locking shot will probably just cock the waggler but not take it down as deep in the water as it should normally sit. Ideally, you want half an inch of the tip of the waggler to show. To achieve this, you'll have to put more shot down the line to sink the waggler that little bit further. Shot on the line also helps the hook bait to sink in a gentle, unsuspicious manner.

You can also fish a waggler with the bait hard on the bottom. To do this, I like to place a larger shot 3–4in (7.6–10.1cm) away from the hook. The fish will lift the shot when it takes the bait and the waggler will rise in the water before shooting under. This method is good for bream, carp and tench.

Dave is nicely set up. He's fishing the stick float very sensitively down a steady run of water.

THE ULTIMATE GUIDE TO FISHING

Stillwaters are rarely still. A light breeze or wind on the water creates currents and surface drift. You may find that the waggler will start to be pulled steadily under the surface of the water. Often, this is because the surface drift pushes the line into an arc and creates pressure on the delicate float. The best way to combat this is to sink your line. When you cast out, plunge your rod tip under the surface and reel in a few times until the line sinks all the way to the float. This should solve the problem.

You can also use a waggler to show a bite when you're stalking fish. Move round the shallows of the lake, especially where there are reeds or fallen trees. Often, you'll see fish feeding — bream, carp and tench are the obvious examples — and simply cast a bait out into the activity. In shallow water, it's often a good idea to let your float lie flat on the surface of the water rather than cock it. Fish can be wary of a cocked float close to their backs. Bites are simply signalled by the float half cocking and then moving off across the water's surface.

On rivers, the most commonly used floats are the stick float and the Avon float. The stick float is for lighter river fishing. It's placed on the line both at the top and bottom and has a slightly bulbous head for buoyancy. Once again, the aim is to shot the stick float down until only the tip shows. Mostly, you spread the shot down the line — almost like buttons on a shirt.

The whole concept of a stick float is to work a steadily paced piece of water in front of you with great care and concentration. This is the ideal method for river roach, barbel, bream and chub. Most stick-float fishing is done with smaller baits such as casters and maggots. Feed the swim steadily with small amounts of loose bait. Place the feed a little upstream so that the current takes it to where your stick float is fishing your own bait.

One of the great skills of stick-float fishing is what we call holding back. As the float moves down your swim, make sure that it rises a little in the water. Below the surface, this is exactly what the bait will be doing, too. As its passage through the water is checked, the bait will flick upward. This often induces a take from a big roach.

Stick-float fishing is all about working close, using light tackle and a little sensitivity. If you want to search longer stretches of water with bigger baits then the float to go for is an Avon. This float is fixed on the line by small elastic float bands at the top and at the bottom. Most of the shot is bulked midway between the float and the hook. Since the float has a buoyant bulb just beneath the tip, the current does not unduly affect it. It also has the ability to suspend large bait, such as a large pinch of bread flake, a lobworm or even a piece of luncheon meat.

The bonus of an Avon float is that you can work it downriver at distances upward of 260ft (80m).

Roach maestro, Mark Everard, trots a stick float on a lovely glide.

Look for backwaters such as this beautiful spot, especially where there's lots of vegetation around. Lilies and rushes are particularly attractive to carp and tench.

The benefit is that you can search out vast areas of river and therefore stand more chance of finding fish. It's a great method for chub, but you've got to keep in constant contact with the float. If you don't, the line will belly in the current and when you do get a bite, you won't be direct to the float and have any power in your strike. You have to mend the line. This means constantly tightening the line so that you're in direct contact with the float and that the line from your rod tip to the float is as straight as possible. It's hard to long trot in winds that are moving across the river. A wind going straight up or straight down is much easier to handle. If you can wade out a little bit on shallows, so you're directly above the float, you'll find control is easier.

At first, it's best to work your Avon float at distances no greater than 65–98ft (20–30m). Working at this distance allows you to practise and ensure your float control is perfect at all times. As you gain in confidence, increase your distance by a couple of feet with each cast.

When you strike, especially at distance, keep it going right over your shoulder until you contact the fish. Over long distances, a mere flick of the wrist won't set the hook. When a fish is hooked, immediately swing your rod tip parallel to the surface of the water to keep the fish down and stop it from boiling on the top. If you do this correctly, you'll avoid scaring the shoal and pick up more fish on subsequent casts.

LEAD AND FEEDER FISHING
ON STILL AND MOVING WATER

Both a lead and feeder will get your bait down to the bottom where a lot of the fish do most of their feeding. Since you have no float, obviously you'll need to think about bite indication. A bite is frequently registered on the rod tip. If you're fishing for sensitive fish, then a quiver tip will highlight the bite more dramatically. However, you can also use a butt indicator on stillwaters just hold the line between the reel and the bottom ring of the rod between your fingers. Feeling for a bite like this is called touch legering and it's particularly effective on rivers.

A flat lead on the river will allow you to hold bottom right in the danger zone. A rolling lead allows you to search the swim.

Touch legering in a nutshell. Hold the rod nice and easily in one hand and the line between the reel and the butt ring in the other. Bites are generally quite distinct plucks on the line.

Let's begin with rivers. Most often, you'll use a straightforward lead. A round lead allows you to roll your bait along the bottom of the river where there are not too many snags and weed. A flattish lead anchors the bait, which is a good technique if you're sure you're right on the fish. There are several rules. First, make sure that you know exactly where

you want your bait to be. The more you splash about with a lead, the more you'll spook the fish and ruin the swim. Think very carefully and try and make your first cast count. If the first cast goes in exactly where you want it, leave the bait there for as long as it takes to get a bite.

Take into account the flow of the river. Let's say there is a tree just downstream of you on the opposite bank and you want to put your bait under it. There's no point casting straight to the spot because the force of the river will simply push it downstream and into the middle of the river. You're far better off casting upstream a little bit so that the flow of the river takes the lead and the bait downstream to settle in the right area close to the tree. If you're using a quiver tip or your straightforward rod tip, put the rod on a rest and angle it at about 90 degrees out across the river. A bite will probably be a series of plucks followed by a big pull. However, it's best to strike at anything positive that is suspicious.

If you're going to touch leger, point the rod more directly toward the bait and have the rod tip closer to the water's surface. Then hold the rod in your striking hand loop the line round the fingers of your reel-winding hand and feel for some indication of a fish taking the bait. Generally, a good indication is

You can fish more lightly and more sensitively with the current behind you.

a pull, but sometimes the line falls slack. The best baits to use with a straightforward leger are large ones such as bread flake, luncheon meat or pellets.

On rivers, most feeder work is done with a closed feeder rather than an open feeder. This is a perfect way to fish maggots in a river because you get them right down to the riverbed and this is where the bigger fish are going to be looking for them. If you simply hand-feed maggots into the river, there's always the chance that they will simply get washed away in the current or eaten by minnows and other small fish.

Sometimes it's important to get out into the river to get the very best position for your feeder rods.

A super barbel that fell for feeder-fished maggots.

Use a closed-faced feeder exactly as you would a normal lead. Simply pack the feeder with maggots and put two or three maggots on your hook. For most river work – for chub or barbel – a size 12 hook with three maggots is a good starting point.

Always try to match the weight of the feeder or the lead with the power of the current. If the lead or feeder is too light, it will get washed away. If it's too heavy, it will cause unnecessary splash and spook more fish. It's a case of trying to strike a balance between the two. It's best to start light and increase in weight until you find that your feeder or lead is remaining exactly where you want it and resisting the force of the current.

You don't have the same problem in still waters. You can use closed feeders with maggots in just the same way as you would in rivers. However, an open feeder comes more into its own on stillwaters. Pack your open feeder – generally called a cage feeder –

with your ground bait, which contains samples of the hook bait. You then have a tail – the distance between the feeder and the hook – of around 12in (30cm) or so. The idea is that when your feeder hits the water and falls to the bottom, the bait in it spills out around your hook and attracts fish in, encouraging them to feed on the bait and to take your hook bait.

Generally, an indication of a bite will be on a quiver tip. Position your rod so that the quiver tip is close to the water's surface, again at about a 90-degree angle to where your swim feeder is lying. Then reel in and tighten the line until there is a slight curve in the tip. Bites can take many forms. Sometimes the tip will simply shiver. Other times it will pluck or bend right round. Sometimes the curve in the tip will actually straighten out and the tip will fall back straight. This generally indicates a fish picking up the bait and swimming toward you, thus relieving the tension on the line. Once again, strike at anything that indicates that the tip is doing something abnormal.

Sometimes, especially on stillwaters, you can use either feeders or leads in conjunction with a butt indicator. Simply put your rod on two rod rests and hang a weight of some sort on the line between the reel and the bottom ring. This can be as simple as a piece of pressed bread! However, most people use shop-bought indicators for this purpose. The modern name is a "hangar". If you use a hangar in conjunction with an electronic bite indicator, you'll have the sound of a take as well as a visual sighting. This means that you can relax a little bit and fish more than one rod.

A modern development on the swim feeder front – for stillwaters more often than rivers – is the method feeder. It's a simple technique but extremely effective. A comparatively large coiled feeder is packed with stiff ground bait in which you press food items. The hook bait is hidden in the ground bait and the whole ball is cast out into the lake or reservoir. Since the method feeder is heavy, long distances can be achieved. Fish will frequently hear the splash and associate it with food. As a result, bites can come relatively quickly. Fish become less cautious as they compete with each other for the bait and frequently the bite is a massive one. The fish more often than not hooks itself against the weight of the feeder itself. This is a great method for bream, carp and tench and the best baits are maggots, pellets, sweetcorn and even small boilies. Do stay close by your rod – if you don't, you'll run the risk of it disappearing into the lake!

A fantastic barbel caught on a rolling lead using a big piece of luncheon meat as bait.

POLE FISHING BASICS

Using a pole gives you distinct advantages over the conventional rod-and-line set up in some situations. Where pole fishing really comes into its own is when you want to fish very tight to snags and set your float and bait with complete accuracy. On many commercial fisheries, carp get used to pressure and you'll find them hanging very close to reed beds, fallen trees and other snags. A pole allows you to fish consistently in this danger zone.

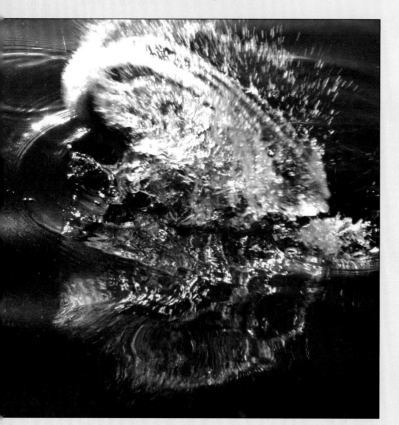

When you're pole fishing, try to avoid fish splashing on the surface and disturbing shoal mates in shallow water.

What are the most important considerations if you're going to use a pole? First and most important, always look up and around you before you set your pole together. Never fish if you're anywhere near electricity cables. This could prove the most important lesson of this entire book.

When you're choosing your pole, don't go all out for length at first. Stick with poles of 32ft (10m) or less if you're new to pole fishing. In most situations, a 19.7ft (6m) pole will do all you need, especially on commercial fisheries.

When you buy a pole, always have it fitted with an elastic in-pole set-up. You're far better getting your local tackle dealer to fix this for you and show you how to do it in the future. You might have to pay a small fee, but the lesson is invaluable. The in-pole elastic technique gives you much more flexibility and a better chance of landing fish.

When you're setting up, prior to a session with the pole, always make sure that you're on a solid, level base. You need your seat box to be absolutely secure or you won't be able to maintain the control over the pole that you need. This is especially true once you fish at distances more than 16.5ft (5m). Ensure all your gear and bait is close to hand so you don't have to stretch for your bits and pieces.

Always look behind you, too. In many cases remember you're going to have to slide your pole back, unshipping sections as you do so if you're playing a better fish. You don't want a passer-by tripping on your pole or a wall causing an obstruction.

When you put your pole together, ensure that the sections fit securely. If they come apart when you're playing a fish, pieces of your pole will disappear into the lake! The best way is to push the sections together and then give each one just half a twist to lock it.

Pole fishing is all about accuracy and control. One of the great benefits is that you can ground the bait with pinpoint precision using a pole. Simply fix a small pole pot to the end of your pole to carry ground bait to your target area. This looks much like an eggcup and you can fill it with 20 pellets or pieces of corn or even some ground bait. It's then easy to simply reverse the pole over the precise spot and all your bait falls in. Although it seems that you're not putting a lot of bait in your pot, if you fill it with every cast you'll find that you're gradually building up a really well-fed swim.

Today, a lot of pole fishing is done on commercial waters where decent carp come along with regularity. When you're playing a fish on a pole, the technique is different to the normal rod-and-line approach. Rather than holding your pole up in the air, try to keep the pole tip almost parallel with the water. Only raise the pole when it's time to net the fish or to swing a small one into hand. If you push the pole up, you increase the pressure on the carbon walls and risk breakages. This is why the pole has the elastic running through it. The elastic stretches under pressure and cushions the power of a running fish.

Always look after the sections of your pole. It's very easy for a section to blow into the water when you're not looking. Equally, it's easy for someone to tread on a pole if you put the sections down in a potentially dangerous place. When you're packing up and taking the pole down it's always good to give each of the sections a quick wipe over. You don't want any grit or sand getting into the joints because this quickly leads to wear, tear and irreparable damage.

CARP FISHING BASICS

Remember that you do not always have to fish for carp using the most up-to-date modern rigs and bait. It's still possible to fish for carp with floats and ordinary bait such as bread and sweetcorn — just as you would for tench or bream. It's possible to use an 11ft (3.4m) Avon-type rod, fixed spool reel and 10lb (4.5kg) line with a size 4 hook and a piece of floating crust. In many waters, carp look for food on the surface. This very simple rig will catch a number of fish.

Success. Gems (left) holds a magnificent common carp while Karim (right) shows off a sleek mirror carp. Notice the forceps — have them close by to get that hook out quickly and easily.

Floating bread is one of the most successful baits.

Alan knows all about stalking for carp. Keep low and hidden so you don't spook the fish.

Lee puts the finishing touches to a perfect set up. His rods and reels are in perfect alignment and the indicators are ready to go. Notice the landing net and the carp mat, where a hooked fish can be laid.

One tip is not to strike too quickly. Wait until the carp has properly sucked down the crust and moves away with it, tightening the line to your rod tip. Then lower the rod, wind tight and strike firmly back upward. It's hugely exciting and very effective.

Carp fishing is a very specialised branch of coarse angling and there are many people who do nothing else — read on for some basic guidelines.

The most important point of any carp fishing is location. Any lake can be hard if you're not on the fish. It's good to keep your eyes open and look for fish either on the surface or throwing up clouds of silt. It pays to be aware of the wind. Carp like to move where a fresh wind is blowing.

One obsession with a lot of carp fishing is the idea of distance, but remember that you can get carp a lot closer in, even along the margins, if you're quiet. It's a good idea to Google any water you're thinking of fishing in, so you can get an idea of where the gulleys and the bars are. Look for snags, such as fallen trees, too, because they will always hold fish as well. But remember to be careful. If a big fish takes line and gets into the snags it's always lost.

Use a spod to get bait out accurately if you're carp fishing at range. The spod is loaded with bait — generally boilies — and cast to where the hook bait will eventually lie.

Try to keep rigs as simple as possible. Never overcomplicate things. The simplest of bolt rigs is all that you're generally going to need and even a running lead, such as the one you would use on stillwaters for bream, will often catch you fish. So don't be put off by the complexity. A main line of between 12 and 15lb (5.5 and 6.8kg) is generally sufficient for carp fishing. If you're fishing in snaggy areas or over a rocky bottom, a 20lb (9kg) or even 25lb (11.3kg) line is safer.

It's a common fault among carp fishers to use too much bait. Sometimes you'll see guys put out bucket loads. This is expensive and often unnecessary unless there are scores of large carp about. If you're fishing for a long session, possibly 8.8lb (4kg) of bait will suffice. The bait will be either boilies or pellets as discussed in the bait chapter. If you're not there for a long-stay session, then it will be quite enough to get 30–40 boilies out by catapult.

Obviously, other baits, such as hemp and pellets work for carp, but a problem can be attracting other fish into the area such as bream and tench. If you

A really good carp boils before the net.

stick to large boilies, then carp are likely to be your main quarry.

In carp fishing, care of the fish is absolutely paramount. It's important that you have an unhooking mat close by you on which to lay any fish after landing. Make sure the carp has recovered before letting it go, especially at night.

DEAD BAIT FISHING

All predators can be caught on dead bait, but especially pike. Dead baits are good when the water is cold and above all when it's coloured. This is when pike begin to hunt, mainly through their acute sense

Ian has flicked out a small dead bait to drift down with the current generated by a weir pool. The day is dark and cold — it could just be that a predator doesn't want to chase a swift-moving lure.

of smell. That's where a big smelly bait on the bottom works better than almost any other bait.

The choice of dead bait is very important. Dead sea fish are particularly effective. My own favourites are probably herring, mackerel, smelt, sprat and sardine — in that order. The problem with sardines is that they are soft. Unless they're frozen, you can't really cast very far with sardines. Other great bait include dead roach, perch and even sections of eel. You can make dead bait more attractive by dyeing them different colours or flavouring them with different oils. Sometimes, if you pack polystyrene into the body of a dead bait, it will float enticingly

off the bottom and appear even more attractive to a passing predator.

Bite indication is important because even the biggest pike don't always grab the bait and bolt off with it. My own advice is to fish a dead bait under a float so you get an immediate indication of when it has been engulfed. Always use the wire trace so that the pike's teeth don't cut through ordinary nylon. Care of the pike is absolutely vital because fish will often swallow dead bait very quickly. You've got to strike as soon as you see any indication of a take. It's also a good idea if you flatten down the barbs on the treble hooks.

Place your dead bait in the sort of places that you'd expect pike to be lying. Search out dying weed beds, overhanging trees and any other obvious ambush point. If you're fishing a pit, work the contours and look for drop-offs and deep gulleys. If you're not getting runs, keep experimenting with the type of the bait and the positioning. Sometimes it's tempting just to sit back and wait. However, most of the time you're better off really working at it to get some exciting sport.

Another way to fish dead bait is "sink and draw". This is the simplest way of fishing, but one of the most effective and most exciting. Simply tie a wire trace with a couple of trebles onto your line and then attach your dead bait with the top treble through its head and the bottom somewhere in the back, close to the dorsal fin. Cast the bait out and let it flutter down toward the bottom. When it has reached the bottom, lift your rod tip and reel in a 3.2ft (1m) or so of line. This will lift the bait from the bottom. When you stop reeling, it will then slowly drop back down again. Repeat this up and down, see-saw motion, until the dead bait is retrieved all the way to your own bank. Wear Polaroid glasses so that if the water is clear, you can see into it and observe if any pike are following. If they are – and it's an exciting moment to see – either try speeding up the rate of retrieve to provoke an instant attack or stop retrieving altogether so the bait sinks down to the bottom. There it might be picked up. Both methods

Ian lets his dead bait drift among the rocks.

Ian isn't afraid to let his dead bait move in the critical areas. There are plenty of snags about, but Ian knows this is where the predators lurk.

work equally well. Experiment until you find which is the better approach for you.

One advantage of sink and draw is that you explore lots of new water. And of course, in winter weather you keep warmer than you do just sitting back and watching the world around you.

LURE FISHING

Lure fishing is the skill of convincing big predators, especially pike, that artificial creations of metal, plastic and wood are real. You've got to work at

this skill. You've got to use imagination. On your retrieve, you've got to make your artificial look and behave exactly like a dying or injured fish. Once you lose concentration, your efficiency will slip. This is why lure fishing is so exciting and popular. It's one of the forms of coarse fishing where you've got to concentrate the most.

You've certainly got to think where to look for your fish. Reed margins, snags, overhanging trees – anywhere a big predator would lurk and mount an ambush. Your casting has got to be spot on, too. That's why often a short rod of 7–8ft (2.1–2.4m)

THE ULTIMATE GUIDE TO FISHING

just gives that extra degree of control. You could try different types of casts — overhead, side flicks and underarm lobs. Remember, the closer you get your lure to the pike, the bigger the chance of a hit.

Lure fishing is also popular because it is simple. Rod, reel, line, wire trace and artificial lure means you're in business. Don't forget swivels on your line. You'll need at least one, or your main line will twist and become useless.

So what types of lures are available to use? Spinners are great. They have an angled blade and a propeller mounted on the central shaft. You retrieve the spinner, the water resistance builds up and the blade rotates, which sends flashes throughout the water. Spinners are excellent lures on bright days.

Spoons are simply pieces of sheet metal hammered so that they wobble and kink their way through the water. You work them very much in the same way that you do spinners. Spoons are generally heavier, which makes them good for deeper water.

Most plugs are made of metal, plastic or wood. My advice is to start with half a dozen models that work close to the surface in midwater and deep water. Buy recognised, popular models and you won't go far wrong. If you're not catching close to the surface, then put on a shallow diver. These work at roughly 6.6–13.2ft (2–4m). If they don't succeed, put on a deep diver, which can often go down as deep as 32ft (10m) or more. This way you're fishing the entire water column.

My own personal favourites are rubber lures. These are made out of soft, rubber plastic and come in all sorts of colours, shapes and sizes. The key is that they move exactly like a small fish through the water. Since they are so soft, they feel like the real thing when an enquiring predator grabs hold of them. I also like the fact that they are frequently equipped with a single hook, which makes unhooking that much easier. Rubbers also really exercise your imagination. You can retrieve. You can jig, which means moving the rod tip up and down so that the rubber flutters vertically in the water. You can even let it settle on the bottom and give it the odd twitch. In fact, the world of rubber is virtually inexhaustible. Another bonus is that rubber fish are cheaper than plugs and spoons.

Rubber lures are great for perch as well as pike.

Lure fishing works better in clear water rather than cloudy water. Ensure that as many casts as possible actually work some type of water feature, for example, an island a reed bed or sunken boat. Lures sometimes work when they are pulled back across open water, but not very often. Always keep contact with your lure and ensure you're in direct control. Sometimes a pike can engulf a lure and you won't have a clue about it if your line is slack. Keep experimenting with the size, action and colour of the lures you use. That's why building up a collection is such a good idea — you've got more options from which to choose.

You'll need a boat to fish lures in areas that you just can't reach from the bank. Always wear buoyancy aids and never go out afloat on your own in rough weather.

Always stick to a plan when you are lure fishing. Check all your equipment is sound and in good working order. Ensure that the hooks are sharp and the knots are strong. It often pays to cast three times to the same spot. The first cast actually wakes up the predator and alerts it to food in the area. The second cast focuses the attention of the predator on the lure that you're retrieving. The third cast actually forces the predator into making its move. Often it does so explosively, so you'll need to stay focused.

When you want to unhook a pike, you've got to be careful of its sharp teeth. Put the pike on a soft, dampened unhooking mat. Kneel down and straddle it with your legs so that it cannot wriggle free. Put a glove on your left hand (if you're right handed) and hold the pike underneath its gill flap. The mouth will open if you then pull the head back. With your right hand gloved if you wish, take a long pair of sharp forceps, locate the lure and the hook or hooks and gradually work them loose. This way there should be no blood at all – either from your own fingers or the fish itself. Try to get the pike back into the water as quickly as you can to avoid further stress.

Remember, if you don't lay the pike on something soft it will start to suffer. If it begins to wriggle about all the fish will do is injure itself. Remember, too, that by pulling the head back as I've described, the mouth will open and you can get to work on the dentistry. Take your time. Stay cool. Practice will make you an expert.

Proof of the pudding. A magnificent pike has just taken a surface-fished lure in an explosion of spray.

A glove and forceps are vital accessories when unhooking pike.

CARE FOR THE FISH AND GENERAL CONSERVATION

A good fisherman cares for his fish and loves his fishery. These are general guidelines, so let's make a list and try to follow them at all times. I'm not saying this is all you need to know about conservation but at least these ideas will get you started. Perhaps they will focus you on developing your own.

• Always use barbless hooks if at all possible. Barbless hook are much safer for the fish and much safer for your fingers or face in case of an accident during the cast.

• Ensure that your landing net has soft mesh and is big enough for the fish you're pursuing. A large, soft, wet unhooking mat is much kinder on the fish once it has been landed.

• If you can, unhook a fish in the water. Ensure that you have forceps or a disgorger to hand.

A lovely carp is nursed back to full health.

A magnificent, fully scaled common carp deserves a gentle release.

• If you want the fish for photographs, be quick with the camera. It's the same if you want to weigh a fish — make sure the scales are set up and ready.

• Always hold a fish with wet hands and don't grip it too tightly. Never hold a fish too far from the unhooking mat in case it squirms out of your grasp.

• Support your fish in the water until it's fully recovered and ready to move off. This is especially important in a river. If the fish swims away too quickly, it can turn over and die.

• Avoid using keep nets. Sometimes a keep sack is useful for a big fish until it recovers.

• Don't hack back branches and reeds to make for easier fishing. Every so often a modest bit of "gardening" is acceptable but ensure nothing drastic spoils the bankside.

• Remove all rubbish that you find on the bank — yours and anyone else's. If everybody does this, all our fisheries will be absolutely spotless.

• Never leave line in trees if you can avoid it. It could entangle birds and wildlife.

• Report dead fish if you see them in any large numbers. Look out for signs of pollution, too. For advice and/or assistance, call the Environment Agency on 0370-850-6506 and explain the problem. You might just save a fishery.

Fly-fishing

Fly-fishing is an ancient form of angling, dating back to the third century. However, the major developments in tackle and techniques have taken place during the last century. Previously considered a sport for the aristocracy, who fished the chalk streams of southern England the pursuit of stocked trout using fly-fishing tackle became available to the masses during the mid-1950s as new reservoirs were constructed to supply the developing urbanization of Britain. No doubt the boom in stillwater fly-fishing for stocked trout continued in the 1960s and 1970s, but it was Blagdon Lake, which nestles in the Mendip Hills of Somerset, that became the first day-ticket stillwater in England opening its doors on 21 May 1904 to a maximum of eight rods per day.

The elitist image that fly-fishing suffered in the past has now all but disappeared, especially with the surge in stocked small stillwaters — the fly-fishers' equivalent of a golfers' driving range. Heavily populated with stock fish that are introduced on a frequent basis, these venues — often referred to as "put and takes" — provide reasonably priced sport that can be enjoyed across the country. Even London can offer something for the fly-fisher in the form of Walthamstow Reservoir, which is stocked with trout by a fish farm located in Devon and Syon Park near Richmond.

Fly-fishing opportunities have also spread to moving water through schemes such as the West Country Angling passport, which delivers day-ticket fishing to the public on a host of venues. Many of these rivers provide wild brown trout fishing, but even salmon and sea trout are available for those keen on migratory fish. These species — widely referred to as "game fish" due to their popularity at the table — have recently made way for coarse fish, such as carp and pike and saltwater species, such as bass during a growth in alternative fly-fishing tactics.

In its most pure form, fly-fishing is designed to mimic the diet of the target fish through the imitation of crustaceans, insects or whatever the quarry may feed upon. This is achieved by attaching fur, feather and associated artificial materials to a hook during a process known as fly tying. The replica is then cast with a series of well-timed, coordinated casting strokes — key factors that differentiate fly-fishing from other forms of angling. It is the elegant casting requirement and subtle fish-catching tactics that are best summed up by the phrase "the gentle art", a common term used to describe the uniqueness of fly-fishing.

The distinctive qualities of fly-fishing continue with the tackle. Casting with conventional weights and fixed spool or multiplying reels filled with monofilament line is not possible. Instead, a thick fly line is used as a casting weight to present the fly. This is attached to a length of fine monofilament called a leader. It is this relatively primitive approach that has earned fly-fishing a widely respected reputation as one of the most sporting methods of angling.

FISH SPECIES

THE WATERS IN WHICH THEY LIVE, THE BAIT,
AND THE TECHNIQUES USED TO CATCH THEM

A delighted angler cradles a well-conditioned small stillwater rainbow trout prior to releasing the fish.

An understanding of what type of fish you are catching with fly-fishing tackle is vital for success. Without this knowledge, it is impossible to cast a line effectively. From the amazing journey of a wild Atlantic salmon to the sometimes bizarre behaviour of stocked rainbow trout, all must be studied to understand their habitat, characteristics and above all, weaknesses.

The most popular fish pursued by fly anglers are from a family called the Salmonids. The different species in this family are many and varied, but all display a small nonfunctional fin on the back, near to the tail. This fleshy nodule, known as the adipose fin, is present in species such as trout – a sporting game fish widely associated with fly-fishing tactics.

Rainbow trout

The striking rainbow trout is not indigenous to Europe but originates from North America. They are a head of wild fish to be found in the Derbyshire Wye, although the majority of rainbow trout are intensively farmed. Forming the base stock of many commercial fisheries, rainbow trout offer easily accessible game fishing and are popular among fishery owners due to their ability to grow quickly.

Stocked rainbow trout often display a voracious appetite, which can cause sudden outbursts of aggression. Many anglers like to deceive rainbow trout using brightly coloured lures as a result of this behaviour. The pink flash down either side of the rainbow trout's flank makes this species instantly

FLY-FISHING

64

recognisable, although the marking varies in intensity from fish to fish. Resident rainbow trout that evade capture after being stocked in a reservoir often become silver, while all have heavily spotted tails. As there is no need to provide time for the fish to reproduce in the form of a close season, it is possible to fish for this species on most European venues throughout the year.

Brown trout

A native species to Europe, the brown trout is one of the most sacred of all fish pursued with fly-fishing tackle. Varying enormously in appearance from location to location, the most highly prized specimens are sometimes the smallest. Residing in tiny moorland streams, these slow-growing wild trout are often trapped between waterfalls or rapids, spending their lives feeding on what little fly life is available. A close season is imposed to protect stocks and allow spawning. The actual time of the close season varies depending on the region.

Indigenous wild brown trout, such as those found in the West Country of England are stunning fish that display a flank covered with spots that are so radiant they look as if they have been hand painted. The spots are predominantly black and contrast beautifully with a few red spots. These breathtaking markings are completed with an unmistakable butter yellow belly and pelvic fins edged in white.

There are abundant opportunities available to catch sizeable brown trout in rivers across Europe, but many specimens are taken while fishing large lowland reservoirs such as Chew Valley Lake in England. Reservoir trout can appear quite different to the wild fish, taking on a silver livery peppered with huge black spots. Small stillwaters also stock brown trout, but these farm-bred fish rarely attain the beauty of a wild or reservoir-grown specimen.

A perfectly formed wild brown trout does not have to be big to provide satisfying sport on fly-fishing tackle.

THE ULTIMATE GUIDE TO FISHING

Hybrid trout

Intensive fish farming has resulted in several trout hybrids that have become particularly popular on small stillwaters. Blue trout and golden trout are genetically identical to the rainbow trout, but the hybrids are quite different in appearance. The blue trout displays an unmistakable silvered flank and a bright blue back, coupled with an ability to put up a strong fight. The golden trout is highly unusual in appearance — the distinctive pink stripe of a rainbow trout clashes with a bright yellow body. There are several other hybrid trout, but one of the most popular is the tiger trout. This hybrid is achieved by fertilizing the eggs of a female brown trout with milt from a male brook trout.

Sea trout

Sea trout are migratory brown trout. They are often described as "enigmatic" thanks to their silent movement upstream during darkness — a period when many nocturnal anglers can be found trying their luck. Slow, meandering pools flanked by dense vegetation is the preferred habitat of the sea trout, so it is advisable to stock plenty of spare flies to replace

The tiger trout is a popular hybrid that display a distinctive livery.

Sea trout provide exciting sport for the nocturnal angler.

for those lost in the branches during a night time session.

Genetic tests show no biological difference between sea trout and resident brown trout, which is reflected in their appearance after returning from the ocean. Sea trout enter the river with a chrome silver flank, big black spots and a black tail. After only a relatively short time, the fish starts to change back into the colours associated with a brown trout.

Sea trout are famed for their hard-fighting qualities and ability to take flies with a rod wrenching pull that often results in nothing more than a sudden rise in the angler's heart rate! Sea trout that are hooked regularly leap clear of the water, providing an adrenalin rush that's responsible for the cult like status that these fish have achieved among anglers.

Hybrids, such as this blue trout offer the small stillwater angler some variety.

THE ULTIMATE GUIDE TO FISHING

Atlantic salmon

An Atlantic salmon hooked on fly tackle is quite an adversary, displaying a powerful fighting ability in the fast-flowing rivers in which it lives. Widely regarded as the "king of fish", this migratory species is noble and resilient – qualities that help it endure an arduous life cycle. After hatching in a well-oxygenated river, the young salmon, known as parr, will spend up to two years feeding in this environment. Following a change into smolt, the juvenile fish head to sea for the first time. Those that return after just one winter away are usually less than 8lb (3.6kg) and referred to as grilse. Fish that manage successive winters grow to much larger weights and return as salmon. Cocks (males) can be distinguished from hens (females) because they have a pronounced lower jaw, called a kype. Sadly, many salmon die after spawning, although some hens do manage repeated journeys, returning to the ocean as kelts.

Sporting a magnificent silver livery, blue-green back and large black spots above the lateral line, this powerful fish uses its forked tail to propel itself back up the river of its birth to spawn. Many changes take place while the salmon is in fresh water, however, because of its difficult journey and refusal to feed. The hen fish lose their silver sheen and become much darker. The cocks take on a blotchy red and orange appearance, which is the reason why some anglers call them "red fish" at this stage in the journey. These stale fish are not good to eat and should always be returned to the water whenever possible.

Grilse provide excellent sport on single-handed fly rods.

The sleek body of the salmon assists its journey upriver and this streamlining is put to good use once hooked.

Grayling have a down-turned mouth, which is perfect for feeding on the riverbed.

It is not fully understood why a salmon that has entered a river to spawn, rather than feed, should decide to take a fly, but it is widely accepted that aggression is a key factor.

Grayling

Grayling can be found in many highly oxygenated streams across their native Europe. They can often be observed feeding near to the riverbeds, devouring aquatic insects using their specially adapted mouth. They are also likely to rise from considerable depth to intercept food at the water's surface, providing fly-fishers with many opportunities.

The grayling's scales are much larger than those of the trout and a huge sail-like dorsal fin dominates the unique appearance of this fish. The powerful body is dappled with a rainbow of red and purple, which cover a silvery grey flank. The dazzling colour is finished off with an exquisite diamond-shaped eye, which is edged with gold. This breathtaking livery is perfect camouflage and can make spotting grayling difficult, especially in low-light conditions. Search for the distinctive forked tail gently pulsating in the current and the body will soon transpire.

An underslung mouth is well suited to the deep-water feeding habits of the grayling, which are quite different to those of a trout. In fact, while the grayling does have an adipose fin, it is not a true Salmonid and spawns during late spring. This provides fly-fishers with an opportunity to target grayling when trout and salmon are out of season.

Fly-fishing tactics regularly fool grayling — a species that is instantly identified by the colourful, prominent dorsal fin.

FLY-FISHING TACKLE

Fly lines

Many novice anglers consider the rod to be their most important purchase, but this is certainly not the case when fly-fishing – instead, it is the fly line that should be given much consideration.

A collection of fly lines will be needed to target a range of depths with success.

Fly lines are far thicker than lines used in other fishing methods and with good reason – it's the line that's used as the casting weight. Depending on whether an angler wishes to fish at short range with small flies or at distance with considerably larger patterns will determine the choice of fly line. Fortunately, the options have been simplified by giving each fly line a number that is used to identify its weight. This system was first developed by the Association of Fishing Tackle Manufacturers (ATFM) and is therefore known as the AFTM scale.

Fly lines start at 0 and rise to 15, but there are a few highly specialised lines that exceed either end of the scale. The following guide can be used to help choose a fly line for most situations:

0–3 Featherweight lines. Highly specialised and ideal when casting small flies a short distance when fishing narrow brooks. Of little use in windy conditions and unsuitable for large fly patterns.

4–6 Lightweight lines. Four and five weight lines are the most common weights used to fish small- to medium-sized rivers. In windy conditions, a number 6 line may be required and this is also an ideal weight to use when fishing small stillwaters. Casts medium-sized fly patterns.

7–8 Medium weight lines. These lines should be used when fishing small stillwaters in windy conditions and can be used to cast a variety of fly sizes. Use a number 8 on reservoirs for long-distance casting and when targeting saltwater species such as bass or pollack.

9–11 Heavyweight lines. Thick in diameter, these lines are dense and can achieve long distances with ease when coupled with a good casting technique. Applications may include salmon fishing on large Scottish rivers such as the Tweed.

12–15 Super heavyweight lines. Highly specialist lines that are seldom used to target European species, although the rise in popularity of fly-fishing for coalfish off the Norwegian coast, requiring huge fly patterns, offers itself to these densities.

Fly lines are not continuous in their diameter along their length and the AFTM scale therefore provides a method of distinguishing the taper of a line. The most common example can be seen in the Weight Forward (WF), which has most of its density situated toward the front end of the line. It is paramount to success that the correct line profile and weight is selected prior to fishing, but it's just as important to select the correct density. Fish may be situated near the surface of the water, requiring a fly line that floats. Equally, they may reside at

Fly lines are used as a casting weight to propel the leader and fly to the fish.

midwater, which would require a slow-sinking line called an intermediate. For fish that are well below the surface, a medium or fast sinker will be required. The AFTM distinguishes fly line densities simply as a letter F for "floater", I for "intermediate" and S for "sinker".

During the last decade, there has been much innovation and it's now possible to purchase a fly line that sinks at a given rate (inches per second). Check the fly line packaging for this information, which is presented as follows:

Number 4 Weight Forward Floating Fly Line – WF4F (common colours include orange, yellow, bright green, white).

Number 6 Weight Forward Intermediate Fly Line – WF6I (common colours include green, blue, clear).

Number 8 Weight Forward Sinking Fly Line – WF8S (common colours include dark green, brown, grey, black).

Number 8 Weight Forward Sinking Fly Line sinking at 5 inches / second – WF8S5.

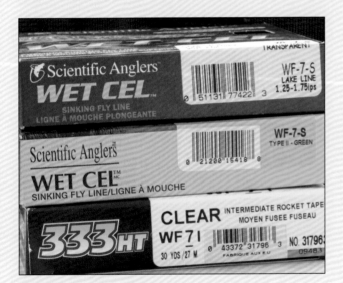

Read the label on the packaging of the fly line box to find out the AFTM code.

Applying a cleaner to the fly line after each use will remove dirt, prolong its life and help with casting.

Fly lines vary in overall design and length, depending on the manufacturer. Most lines are between 89 and 119ft (27.4 and 36.5m) long, which allows for a reasonable casting distance. If a fish is captured and requires more than this standard length, it's necessary to load a base of thin stringlike line, known as backing, onto the reel, to enable the fish to be successfully played.

Fly lines have evolved from materials such as silk, which needed an enormous amount of maintenance. Contemporary fly lines are made from PVC and similar plastics wrapped around a variety of cores. The cores vary depending on manufacturer, but it's worth checking if they are stretch or nonstretch. Purchasing a high-quality fly line with a smooth coating is highly recommended. Cleaning will prolong the life of the line and aid its passage through the rod rings.

Fly rods

The rod is a fundamental piece of equipment and vital to fly-fishing success. Many years ago, cane and green heart were used to construct a flexible rod that was designed to bend under the tension of the fly line. These materials soon gave way to fibreglass which, in turn, was superseded by carbon fibre – the material of choice for most modern fly rods. Carbon fibre rods are lightweight and allow for easy casting over prolonged periods. They also act as an excellent shock absorber while fighting a hooked fish.

A continuous series of casting movements is used to propel the fly to the fish. This process is assisted by the weighted fly line, which flexes the rod. When the rod recoils, the energy stored is transferred into the line. The line travels above the water's surface, carrying with it the leader and fly prior to landing under gravitational pull.

The fly rod is also coded using the AFTM rating and should be balanced with the appropriate fly line. Check just in front of the cork handle for a number that should correspond with the chosen fly line. Length is another important consideration, depending on the fishing environment and fish to be caught. Use the following as a general guide:

5'0" to 6'6" rods/AFTM 0–3: Small rivers surrounded by trees. Short casting with lightweight dry flies and nymphs.

7'0" to 8'6" rods/AFTM 3–5: Small rivers with a little more space to cast. Short to medium range casting with light to medium weight flies.

Use a short rod when fishing wild trout river, because they are often surrounded by vegetation.

A single-hand fly rod provides superb sport on reservoirs, bending throughout when a fish is hooked.

9'0" to 10'0" rods/AFTM 5–7: Light line rods (5/6) used for medium sized rivers such as chalk streams and small stillwaters. Seven weight used for small stillwaters, large reservoirs and bank boat fishing.

10'0" to 12'0" rods/AFTM 8–9: Reservoir fishing in strong wind with large patterns and lightweight salmon.

13'0" to 15'0" rods/AFTM 10–11: Double-handed salmon fishing on large rivers.

Check the fly rod blank to find out the weight of fly line for which it is rated.

THE ULTIMATE GUIDE TO FISHING

Very long casts are possible with two-handed fly rods.

There are various other specialised rods available on the market, but this guide will assist with most freshwater situations.

Handle: Generally, the rod handle is fashioned from cork and is an important section of any rod. A comfortable grip is vital to fly-fishing success and the most expensive rods usually come complete with high-quality cork. There are three main types of grip: the Half Wells, Full Wells and Scroll.

Rod rings: The fly line needs to pass through the rod rings with ease to ensure accuracy and distance where required. Old-fashioned lined rings reduced in diameter along the rods length and hindered the passage of the fly lines, giving way to lightweight snake rings that are used on most modern fly rods.

Fly reels

Coarse and sea fishing require mechanical reels with gears. The fly reel is much simpler. Described as direct drive, few fly reels are geared — one rotation will recover just a few inches of line. This lack of line recovery means that many anglers retrieve their line once a fish is hooked by pulling it in with their hand. You can buy fly reels that incorporate a drag system — a brake that is available in various formats and is usually applied with the assistance of a knob on the back of the reel cage.

Most modern reels are "large arbor" and incorporate a spool to store the fly line in wide-open coils. This helps to reduce line memory, which manifests itself in the form of kinks in the line. The

Large arbor fly reels store lines in wide-open coils and help to reduce line memory.

Serious saltwater fly-fishing should only be approached with a high-quality bar stock aluminium reel.

kinks do not pass through the rod rings easily during casting or lie straight when in the water, leading to much frustration.

All tackle should be balanced and so it is very important to purchase a reel that's not too heavy for the rod. To check if a reel is suitable, attach it to the rod. If the tip of the rod falls to the floor, the reel is too light. If the reel falls toward the floor, then it's too heavy. A carefully selected rod and reel will balance evenly in the hand.

Leaders

Leaders provide an unobtrusive link between the fly and the thick casting weight of the fly line. Choosing the correct fly rod, reel and line is an important process, but it's also essential to select leaders carefully. There are two types available: knotless tapered leaders and hand-tied leaders.

Pressure can be applied to the spool when a fish is fighting by engaging the drag. This is controlled by a knob shown here on the back of the reel.

Knotless tapered leaders: These leaders are available commercially in a variety of lengths and breaking strains – this information is printed on the packet for easy identification. An ingenious piece of technology, knotless tapered leaders take the form of an elongated piece of tapered nylon. The overall simplicity of the knotless tapered leader means that it's the ideal choice for novice anglers, but experienced anglers often find them useful, too. There are many advantages to be gained from knotless tapered leaders, but the main benefit is their ability to transfer energy from the fly line to the fly perfectly (coupled with good casting technique), positioning the artificial fly as far from the fly line as possible. This process is known as good turnover.

line and fly. In addition, the diameter of the leader will also increase to the point that it will no longer be usable, especially when using the very fine leaders required for river fishing with small flies. Finally it's advantageous to fish more than one fly at a time in many fishing situations. Unfortunately, the knotless tapered leader is only suitable for a single fly.

Hand-tied leaders: These leaders require considerably more effort than the knotless tapered variety but provide an angler with a diverse range of opportunities while also saving a lot of money. Created from spools of leader material, it's still possible to taper a hand-tied leader by connecting together various diameters of monofilament with a water knot.

A knotless tapered leader will help to present the fly efficiently when coupled with well-practiced casting techniques.

Store your leaders neatly and keep them close to hand.

However, there are also a few disadvantages. Knotless tapered leaders can be expensive and the attachment of each new fly decreases the length significantly, shortening the distance between fly

The general guide that follows will help you to choose a leader suitable for the environment in which you are intending to fish and the species you are hoping to target.

Hand-tied leaders are created by knotting together a variety of breaking strains, which are stored on spools such as these.

LEADER GUIDE

Knotless tapered leader = KTL
Hand-tied leader = HTL

Rivers

Trout/grayling – KTL: Length 9–12ft (2.75–3.65m)
Breaking strain at point 5–2lb (2.2–0.9kg)
Salmon/sea trout – KTL: Length 7–12ft (2.1–3.65m)
Breaking strain at point 20–10lb (9–4.5kg)

Lakes

Trout – KTL: Length 9–12ft (2.75–3.65m)
Breaking strain at point 10lb to 6lb (4.5 to 2.7kg)
Trout – HTL: Length 10–20ft (3–6m)
Breaking strain at point 10–6lb (4.5–2.7kg)
It's possible to customise hand-tied leaders for many eventualities, but each section of leader would generally be of a similar length. For example, a 15ft (4.6m) hand-tied leader could be constructed as follows: 5ft (1.5m) of 10lb (4.5kg) + 5ft (1.5m) of 8lb (3.6kg) + 5ft (1.5m) of 6lb (2.7kg).

Choosing a leader

Leaders are vital to fly-fishing success, yet many anglers overlook this key element of their tackle. Sometimes just lengthening the leader or lowering the breaking strain will prove successful, although it is not recommended to use a leader that may not be suitable for the size of fish likely to be encountered. Large fish, such as salmon, may break a lightweight knotless tapered leader that's more suited to petite flies and small wild trout. Consider weather conditions, too. A long leader with lots of droppers is asking for trouble in high wind!

Copolymer or fluorocarbon?

There are a number of distinct leader materials on the market, usually split into two key categories: copolymer and fluorocarbon. Copolymer has a fine diameter, is relatively limp and sinks slowly. It's the ideal choice when fishing close to the surface of the water. Fluorocarbon should be used for all subsurface fishing, because it is stiffer and reflects less light than copolymer.

The leader provides an link between the fly line and the fly.

ACCESSORIES

There are many gadgets and gizmos available to fly-fishers, all of which promise to help us catch more fish. Collecting tackle is fun, of course, but fly-fishing is a mobile method of angling and accumulating too much equipment, which has to be dragged to and from the water's edge. A lightweight approach to fly-fishing has many benefits. In particular, it allows a roving style that enables an angler to cover more water than most other methods of fishing. Even so, there are some crucial items of tackle that fly-fishers must carry to ensure an enjoyable experience.

Waistcoat

The waistcoat is the fashionable way of transporting many accessories with ease. Modern "pack-style" waistcoats usually incorporate extra space in the form of a rucksack to carry food, water, spare clothing and other essential items.

Sunglasses

A vital piece of kit, first and foremost sunglasses offer eye protection from the sharp point of a hook. NEVER cast a fly without wearing eye protection. Polaroid sunglasses reduce glare and help an angler to see into the water effectively.

Use a waistcoat to carry essential items of tackle close to hand.

Fly boxes

A growing fly collection is valuable and requires a suitable method of storage. When you choose a fly box, consider how many flies you need to carry. Aim for a box that is water resistant and floats.

Line snips

Scissors or nail clippers can be used to cut line, but I recommend purchasing a purpose-built line snip.

Leader trap

Various products are available on the market to store waste leader accumulated during a fishing session. It is an important conservation consideration, because loose line that strays into the environment can cause wildlife serious injury or even death.

Store flies neatly for easy identification while fishing.

A set of line snips will help you to cut the leader quickly and cleanly when you need it.

Forceps can be used to remove hooks and will cause less damage than fingers when releasing your catch.

Forceps

Useful to retrieve flies from the mouth of a fish after it has been landed and to flatten barbs if releasing fish after capture.

Retractors

These attach to your waistcoat or pack and conveniently store line snips and other essential tools close to hand.

Floatant

Flies that float on the surface are known as dry flies. A dry fly that has been exposed to the water for a period of time sinks as the materials used to construct it become waterlogged. Apply floatant to a dry fly prior to fishing to help maintain buoyancy.

Leader sink

It is important to reduce the natural grease on the fly line using copolymer leader to present dry flies on the water's surface. Use a liquid or paste-sinking agent to cut the leader through the surface film. Do not apply to fluorocarbon leaders.

Bite indicators

These controversial tackle items are similar to the floats used by coarse or sea anglers and help with take detection. Available in many different styles, including yarn and stick on foam, bite indicators attach to the leader to enable fly patterns to be suspended at predetermined depths.

There are many types of bite indicators on the market, including colourful yarn, which can be spliced into a leader.

Net

It is advisable to carry a rotproof knotless mesh net to help land the fish. When purchasing the net, consider the fishing conditions and the species you are likely to encounter. Boat fishing on a reservoir with a long leader will demand a lengthy handle, while landing a large salmon will require an appropriate net. Fish from smaller rivers can be tackled with a short-handled miniature pan net.

Priest

Known as "the priest" because it "administers the last rights", this heavy clublike tool is used to dispatch fish swiftly and humanely with several sharp blows applied to the cranium, just above the eyes. This process may appear brutal to an onlooker, but it's the most humane way available to kill the quarry. Anglers who do not wish to kill their catch may return fish, but it's worth checking to see if a venue allows anglers to practice catch and release.

Marrow spoon

This vital piece of kit resembles an elongated spoon. It is inserted into the mouth of a trout after it has been dispatched. The marrow spoon is pushed down into the stomach, twisted one full turn and then removed. Check the recessed cup to identify what the fish has been feeding on.

Keep important accessories close to hand rather than storing them away in a bag.

THE ULTIMATE GUIDE TO FISHING

Bass bag

A mesh sack with handles designed to store fish and keep them fresh after capture. Place the fish inside, moisten with water from the river or lake and put the bag in the shade. As the water evaporates it will cool the contents.

Wading staff

This is used to provide extra support while wading over uneven surfaces. The wading staff can also be used to test depth prior to wading.

Permits and licenses

The requirements for permits and licenses to fish vary across the world on a regional and local basis. Always find out who owns a stretch of water prior to fishing and obtain a permit. Many countries also require a rod licence. Enquire at local tourist offices, post offices or the local library for further information. The internet also provides many resources for anglers looking for fishing opportunities.

CLOTHING

Fishing is a relaxing pastime and should be fun. It is imperative to maintain a comfortable body temperature to maximise enjoyment. Discomfort results in a lack of concentration. Consider the amount of walking likely to be involved when fishing, the quantity of kit you are carrying and the general climate. Fishing-specific garments that help casting movement often incorporate conveniently positioned storage compartments. Most are fashioned from lightweight, breathable fabrics to avoid excessive perspiration. Footwear should be appropriate to the terrain and well fitted to avoid blisters.

Layering

The most effective way to retain body heat during cold weather is to build up layers of clothing. Start with a breathable base layer consisting of thermal vest

Use layers of clothing to fish during inclement weather.

and tights. Wear a thin pair of socks under a thick pair of socks that are soft and comfortable to walk in. Trousers should be lightweight and close fitting so that they do not crumple up under waterproof trousers or waders. Jeans are not recommended when fishing in cold weather because the fabric is heavy, crumples under the outer layers and lowers body temperatures rapidly if the material becomes wet. Wear a warm shirt and a windproof fleece jacket such as the soft shell fleeces now widely available. Add an additional fleece jacket for extra warmth. If wading in very cool water, consider a set of fleece trousers, similar to jogging pants, that can be worn over thermal tights.

Headwear

Suitable headwear is essential to provide protection from stray hooks and the sun. In cold weather, headwear can help you retain heat. A hat with a brim or peak is also useful when trying to spot fish in the water, because it reduces glare by shielding the eyes from the sun. Cover up well with a high-factor sunscreen during warm weather.

Gloves

There are many specialist gloves for fly-fishing on the market. Neoprene gloves can be very useful in extremely cold weather. Fingerless fleece gloves are highly recommended because they are warm and allow easy movement of the fingers when performing tasks such as knot tying.

Waterproof trousers/bib & brace

Wet weather deters many anglers from a day's fishing but with waterproof clothing it's possible to remain warm, dry and comfortable at the water's edge. Breathable, lightweight, waterproof fishing trousers are readily available, with plenty of pockets for storage. Boat anglers exposed to the elements often use a bib and brace system of waterproof trousers to shield them. Select a size that will allow for layers.

For your own safety, it is essential to wear eye and head protection when casting a fly.

Three-quarter length waterproof jacket/ wading jacket

A warm jacket will compliment a well-chosen set of trousers and should feature similar breathable characteristics. Stillwater fly-fishers frequently opt for a three-quarter-length coat with a sizable hood that can be worn over a hat. Fly-fishers wading in deep water often opt for wading jackets that have a short cut and are designed to be worn over chestwaders. Other important features to look for in a jacket include; D rings to enable easy attachment and transportation of nets/accessories, taped cuffs to reduce water seepage up sleeves and a zipped up front with overlapping poppers that aids insulation and waterproofing.

THE ULTIMATE GUIDE TO FISHING

A high-quality three-quarter length jacket will keep the rain at bay during a lengthy stillwater session.

Waders

There are two main wader styles on the market: thigh and chest. Thigh waders extend well above the knee and are held in position with a strap that is attached to a belt. Chestwaders rise up the torso and are supported by a pair of braces. Chestwaders are the most practical and allow for deep wading, although you must be very careful when wading in very deep, fast-moving water. Always wear a wading belt to slow the entrance of water into the legs in the event of a fall and never wear chestwaders on a boat. Many materials are used in the manufacturer of waders, including rubber and neoprene, but they are rapidly losing popularity in favour of lightweight, breathable fabrics such as Gore-Tex. These waders are a joy to use but require careful maintenance to prolong their life.

Chestwaders offer far more versatility than thigh waders.

Stocking foot waders coupled with wading boots offer a comfortable alternative to traditional chestwaders.

Buoyancy aids are compulsory on most venues offering boat fishing.

Stocking foot waders and wading boots

Modern waders are available in two parts — a fabric trouser attached to a neoprene sock — which is then covered with a shoe similar to a walking boot. This system allows for effortless movement, which is desirable during a day's wading. Since most modern designs feature breathable fabrics, perspiration is also reduced. Wading boots feature a variety of soles including cleats, felt, rubber, studs or a combination. Ensure the boots are comfortable but remember you'll need to purchase one size above your normal shoe size to allow for the neoprene sock. Repair kits incorporating patches and glue are available, similar to the puncture repair kits for bicycle tires, should an accident occur resulting in a tear or puncture.

Buoyancy aid/lifejacket

Sadly, every year there are anglers who fail to return home after a day's fishing because they drown. These accidents are totally unnecessary. Follow these simple rules to stay safe:

1) Always wear an appropriate safety device. Even the most experienced swimmers are helpless against strong currents if they are knocked unconscious during a fall.
2) Never wade in unfamiliar water without testing the depth with a wading staff.
3) Do not wade in fast water if you are unsure and never be over confident in any water.
4) Fish with friends where possible.
5) Carry a mobile phone and a first-aid kit in case of emergencies.
6) Be aware of the possibility of flash floods.

ENTOMOLOGY &
ARTIFICIAL FLIES

ENTOMOLOGY

Many forms of angling rely on baits that emit smell to attract fish. Fly-fishing is different. The idea behind an artificial fly is that it will create the illusion of life, using fur and feather bound to a hook with thread. Flies form a substantial proportion of the diet of nonmigratory game fish species, such as trout and grayling. Each fly species or order can be identified by observing the wings while the fly is at rest. There are four key groups: flat-wing, roof-wing, up-wing and hard-wing flies.

Flat-wing flies buzzers

Flat-wing flies are consumed on a regular basis by trout. In some circumstances this group of flies may total up to 75 percent of the overall diet of the fish. Present throughout the year, flat-wing flies can generate a feeding response in many conditions, especially during the spring and summer months.

Flat-wing flies start life as an egg deposited on the surface of the water, which then sink to the bottom. This stage in the life cycle is of little interest to the trout. Once the egg hatches, it takes the form of a larva, best known as the bloodworm. Before the larva can journey to the water's surface it must pupate; only then can it swim up through the water layers. It's this enticing motion that frequently attracts the attention of the trout. The pupae are eaten in such vast numbers that fly-fishers who ignore this stage in the life cycle will be at a serious disadvantage.

Artificial flies that are designed to imitate the pupae are commonly called "buzzers". This nickname refers to the buzzing sound emitted by the adult fly. Common flat-wing flies of interest to fly-fishers are the Chironomid midges, but land-breeding species

An assortment of flies will be needed to imitate the insects upon which trout feed.

Buzzer pupae are consumed by trout on a regular basis and are therefore frequently imitated by fly anglers.

such as hawthorn and crane flies have particular seasonal importance.

Roof-wing flies – caddis and sedge

Flies that display wings with a rooflike appearance while at rest are commonly called sedge or caddis flies. Caddis flies belong to the order Trichoptera and follow a similar life cycle as the flat wings – starting life as an egg, which hatches as a larva, pupates and then emerges as an adult fly. Caddis larvae are similar in appearance to caterpillars and live in a case formed from materials such as fine gravel. Many fly patterns mimic the cased varieties of caddis, but imitations of free-swimming species and flies that don't make cases do exist and are significantly important to river anglers.

In cased varieties, pupation takes place within the case and the caddis fly releases itself in readiness to swim to the surface. Unlike buzzers, caddis fly pupae are most at risk from predatory fish during this period of metamorphosis. Flies that manage the journey unscathed may hatch into an adult immediately and take to the air soon afterward. Others attract unwanted attention as they attempt to dry their wings on the surface of the water. Sand fly, grannom and caperer are all important examples of caddis flies.

Up-wing flies – mayflies

The seasonal hatch of mayflies during late spring and early summer is a revered event that many river anglers look forward to with great anticipation.

Sporting a distinctive upright wing the mayfly is just one of many species in the order Ephemeroptera that is of interest to fly-fishers. Many specialist books describe the subtle differences between each fly in this order in great detail, but in reality these facts may overcomplicate matters for those accumulating a general knowledge.

Up-wing flies start life as an egg that hatches into an insect form called a nymph. Nymphs vary enormously in size and most are brown, olive or black in colouration. The mayfly nymph is one exception – it's creamy white with brown spots and banding. Trout and grayling prey on the nymphs of up-wing flies in substantial numbers.

Before reaching maturity, the nymph of an up-wing fly splits open its case and emerges as a juvenile stage called a dun. The dun has an opaque appearance but changes when its outer skin divides to reveal a shiny body and crystal clear wings. Known as a spinner, the adult fly is now fully formed and able to mate in midair. The females then deposit their eggs in the water and die – the lifeless wings spread out at right angles to their bodies. This causes a frenzied feeding state as fish gorge upon spent spinners as they plunge to the water. It can be copied with artificial patterns that recreate the silhouette of

This pattern is called a Harry Potter and can be used to imitate a variety of insect life including caddis and sedge.

A stone-clinging nymph that will eventually hatch into an up-wing fly shown beside two imitation patterns.

the fallen insect. There is a huge range of up-wing patterns available but a selection incorporating the key stages of mayflies, dark olives, medium olives and blue-winged olives will cater for most eventualities.

Hard-wing flies – stone flies

Flies vary in significance from region to region and none more so than hard-wing stone flies in the order Plecoptera. These are a valuable addition to the trout's diet and an anglers fly box in areas such as northern England but in other areas there are so few stone flies around that they are not worth copying.

Adult flies can be very large, with a wingspan of over 2in (5cm), but most are much smaller. At rest the distinctly curved wings lie flat along the body and have a scaly appearance, which makes them easy to identify. Willow flies, needle flies and yellow sallies are examples of natural stone flies that an angler may need to imitate.

Identifying diet

A stonefly nymph crawls onto a rock, ready to hatch.

A basic understanding of the four fly orders must be supported by knowledge of other forms of nourishment for the target species. Stillwater trout in particular are presented with an amazing range of food items, which may include damsel nymphs, hoglouse, freshwater snails, juvenile fish and shrimps. All of them can be imitated. Check local fly hatches prior to a fishing session, stocking fly boxes based on venue location and seasonal variations. Turn over rocks, scan the surface of the water and check spiders' webs while fishing for more evidence. Look out for birds, too, such as swallows and swifts, as they feed on hatching flies.

THE ARTIFICIAL FLY
Dry flies and wet flies

The term fly-fishing suggests that anglers are fishing on the surface. However, tactics can be used to mimic many different life-forms both on and below the water's surface. The overall result is that artificial flies have become grouped into two main categories. Wet flies are fished subsurface and dry flies are fished on the surface. Each group is further split into hook sizes that are identified by a number that decreases as the size increases. The main body of the hook can be short or long and is called a shank.

Hook size guide

This guide provides a key to the main hook sizes that apply to fly-fishing.

20–16: Minute short shank patterns mainly used on trout/grayling rivers.

14–10: Small to medium-sized patterns suitable for rivers. Size 12 and 10 short shanks are frequently used when stillwater trout fishing. Long shank size 10 can be used to target salmon.

8–6: Medium to large patterns with some benefit to the stillwater trout fisher. These sizes are regularly used when salmon fishing, in both short and long shank and also for saltwater flies.

4–2: Very large short and long shank hook used

to tie patterns aimed at saltwater species and pike.

1/0–4/0: Enormous pike and saltwater flies tied on long shanks.

Stillwater trout – wet flies

Wet flies imitate a huge array of food that stillwater trout may encounter, including crustaceans, larvae, pupae and bait fish known as fry. The artificial patterns identified below are essential in the collection of every stillwater fly-fisher. It should be noted that some of the suggestions cross over and may be applicable to rivers.

Imitation bloodworm larvae

Often tied on hooks made from heavy wire and constructed using elastics, latex and other similar materials to emulate the wormlike characteristics of a larva. Suggested patterns include the Apps Bloodworm and San Juan Worm in red and olive. Sizes 14, 12 and 10.

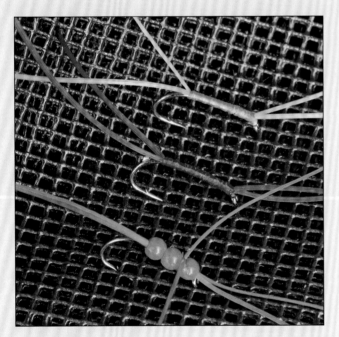

Buzzer pupae begin life as a bloodworm larvae, which have a wormlike appearance.

Imitation buzzer pupae (subsurface)

This stage of the buzzer's life cycle has spawned thousands of unique patterns that may seem incomprehensible. Often tied on curved hooks to imitate the banana-shaped profile of the pupae and incorporating materials that simulate the segmented body, bulbous thorax, wing buds and featherlike breathing tubes. Carry buzzers in a wide range of sizes and colours; black is essential. Suggested patterns include the Red Butt Epoxy Buzzer, Suspender Buzzer and Diawl Bachs. Sizes 14, 12 and 10. Use in size 16 down to 20 on rivers.

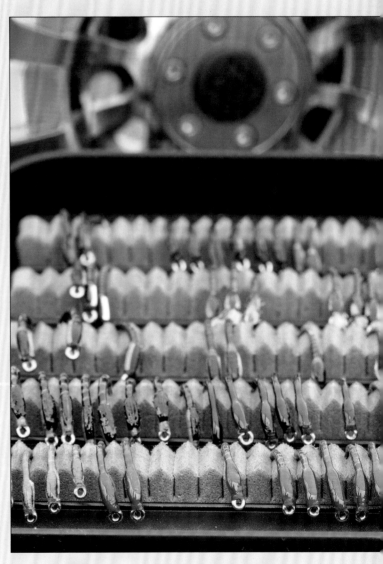

Artificial buzzer pupae patterns such as these stealth buzzers are available in many sizes and colours.

Imitation damsel nymphs

Damsel nymph imitations from the order Odanta are essential in the collection of every stillwater fly-fisher. A large nymph is pale green to olive in colouration. This species moves with an enticing wiggle that trout find extremely hard to resist. Try Flashback Damsels and Classic FMs in short and long shank sizes 12 to 10.

A realistic illusion of life can be created with fur and feather — in this case a damsel nymph.

Imitation Corixa

Late summer and autumn often triggers an explosion of water boatmen commonly called Corixa by anglers. Specific imitations are available; sizes 14 and 12 are of most interest.

Imitation hoglouse

Similar in appearance to the common woodlouse. Hare's-ear Nymph will be taken readily by trout hunting hoglouse. Suggested sizes 14, 12 and 10. Carry in smaller sizes when river fishing to imitate caddis and varied nymphs.

Imitation fish fry

Trout that are preparing for a long winter will begin feeding heavily on small fish fry (where available) during the autumn. Minkies in sizes from 10 to 6 are the most common pattern relied upon to imitate fry.

Stillwater trout – dry flies

Ironically much of the armoury of a fly-fisher is designed to fish subsurface. However, the anatomy of a trout suggests that it will look upward for food, since its eyes are positioned near the top of its head. Therefore it's foolhardy to ignore the dry flies required to fish at the waters surface.

Imitation buzzer pupae (surface film)

A category of artificial flies, known as emergers, are neither true wet flies nor dry flies. Part of the fly sits above the surface film while the rest sits below the water. Use emergers to represent hatching buzzers as they hang just below the surface film. Good examples of emergers applicable to stillwater fly-fishing include the Shipman's Buzzer and Shuttlecock Buzzer in sizes 14, 12 and 10.

This artificial fly, known as Big Black, can be used to imitate a hatching buzzer pupae.

The controversial Blob does not look like any naturally available fish food but still manages to attract fish.

Imitation adult buzzer

Artificial patterns that represent adult buzzers cross over slightly with the emergers. Dry fly patterns are tied to closely resemble the silhouette, relevant size and colour of the adult flies and feature a chicken feather wrapped just behind the eye of the fly to create a spiky collar known as a hackle. The hackle helps to support the fly and provides a strong silhouette. The most important artificial pattern to stock in a fly box is commonly known as a Hopper although a modern pattern known as a Harry Potter is very popular and has gained a huge following. The most popular sizes are 14, 12 and 10.

Imitation daddy longlegs/crane fly

This awkward looking insect emerges in numbers late in the summer and can spark a furious feeding frenzy. Try patterns such as the Detached Daddy in size 10.

Stillwater trout – lures

Fly-fishing imitates fish food in its purist form, but there are many occasions when a brightly coloured selection of fur and feather strapped to a hook will attract interest. Termed lures, these patterns seldom resemble anything that a trout might witness in its natural environment.

Blobs

The most notorious modern-day lure of its time, blobs are loved by some and loathed by others! The blob is so called thanks to its thick body made from a lustrous artificial material known as Fritz. It's available in a huge array of colours although black, fluorescent orange and coral pink are the most popular shades. Size 10 or 8 short shank hooks.

Cat's whiskers

This popular lure is available in a range of colours, although a white wing and tail coupled with a fluorescent yellow body is the most famous version. Sizes ranging from a 10 short shank to an 8 long shank are recommended.

The Humungus is a variation of the famous cat's whiskers.

Imitation nymphs

There are many species of nymphs that can be used depending on the venue. Famous patterns such as the Pheasant Tail Nymph, Hare's-ear Nymph and Copper John provide extremely good suggestive imitations. Stock in varying weights, from size 20 through to 10.

Cormorants

These subtle lures are usually tied on short shank hooks in size 12 and 10. A small clump of Black Marabou forms the wing and Peacock Herl is wound along the shank to create a body. Cormorants are brilliant general purpose patterns that catch in many varied circumstances.

Boobies

This is an extremely adaptable lure that can be tied with a blob-like body or even dressed down to take on the imitative form of a nymph. Boobies are instantly identified by two huge foam eyes (which give the pattern its name) fixed in place just behind the eye of the hook. Carry in size 12 to 10. Under no circumstances should a booby be used when catching and releasing because fish take this fly deep inside their mouths.

RIVER TROUT AND GRAYLING – WET FLIES

Imitation caddis larvae

The larvae of adult caddis flies constitute a reasonable proportion of the diet of a grayling. This species often share their river habitat with trout and regularly tear nymphs and caddis larvae from stones. The down-turned mouth signifies the fish is a bottom feeder. Despite their name, Czech Nymphs are in fact a popular imitation of caddis larvae, utilising materials such as hare's fur covered with latex to mimic the case formed by this bottom-dwelling insect. A variety of weights are useful in sizes from 16 up to 8.

Czech Nymphs can be used to imitate caddis larvae.

Spiders

This group of patterns is used to imitate drowning flies and is characterised by a sparse body and soft, highly mobile hackle. Try Partridge and Orange in sizes 16, 14 and 12.

RIVER TROUT AND GRAYLING – DRY FLIES

Imitation midge

Midges may constitute a high proportion of the diet of a wild river trout, especially on cold upland rivers where food can be in scarce supply. Small, drab flies such as Black Gnats plus F-Flies in black and olive should be stocked in sizes 16 down to 20.

These artificial patterns can be used to copy emerging and fully hatched adults.

A good selection of nymph and caddis larvae patterns.

You may need to match the size of the hatch and this may require minute patterns.

Imitation caddis pupae

Caddis flies or sedge, are important insects that often encourage an impressive rise. The pupae will be consumed during their ascent to the surface, but it's just prior to hatching that they become particularly vulnerable. Klinkhammers are world famous and are widely used to copy hatching caddis flies. In many circumstances, grayling seem unable to resist Klinkhammers and will rise to take them, even when there seems to be no signs of a hatch or feeding fish. Sizes 20 through to 10.

Imitation caddis flies

Adult caddis flies possess a familiar outline that anglers copy with the assistance of many specific patterns tied to represent key species such as the grannom or caperer. The generic Elk Hair Sedge is hard to beat in a range of sizes from 20 to 8.

Imitation up-wing flies

Non specific artificial patterns such as the Adams are used to represent up-wing flies. Choose parachute-style patterns that are tied with a hackle that sits parallel with the hook shank, positioning them in a lifelike manner. Once the natural flies have reproduced, the spent carcasses will fall to the water. It's during this time that anglers fishing with a spent spinner pattern will enjoy success. Sizes from 20 to 10.

Imitation hard-wing flies

Fully developed stone flies are possibly not as significant as flies from the three other groups. However some areas of Europe, such as northern England do enjoy a decent hatch that fish respond to. As a result, it's sensible to carry an appropriate artificial. Sizes 14 to 10.

The Adams is a classic up-wing dry fly imitation.

FLY-FISHING
WATERS AND VENUES

A successful day's fly-fishing relies on well-chosen equipment, knowledge about the diet of your quarry and an awareness of the environment in which they live. Without this understanding we are at a serious disadvantage from the moment we arrive at the water's edge.

Characteristics that form the structure of a venue are known as features in angling terminology. The ability to recognise features within a venue is an important step in the right direction, but this follows an important overall decision regarding the venue itself. The following section describes the many and varied opportunities available, while detailing the key features that the fish are attracted to.

STILLWATER FLY-FISHING VENUES
Small stillwaters

These miniature lakes, which in some cases might be better described as ponds, are ideal practice grounds for every level of angler but, in particular, those who are new to the sport. A large lake can appear daunting at first sight, so smaller stillwaters can provide an excellent opportunity to improve fly-fishing techniques with the added bonus of catching fish. Regularly stocked with trout, often on a daily basis, the slightly artificial nature of these venues is not to every angler's taste, however.

The vast majority of smaller stillwaters are located within easy reach of city centres, so they can become crowded with anglers. As a result, they may not be suitable for those seeking a solitary fishing experience. Most small commercial stillwater fisheries are artificial venues, which allows the designer scope to create an array of exciting features

that offer the fish an environment in which they will feel safe. Fish that are settled in their environment are much more likely to feed, which means they will be vulnerable to a well-presented fly.

Smaller stillwaters are the ideal training ground for novice fly-fishers.

Reservoirs such as this one offer fly-fishers challenging fishing in beautiful surroundings.

Lakes and reservoirs

There are countless opportunities to enjoy lakes and reservoirs across Europe, which provide a real challenge for the flourishing fly-fisher.

Reservoirs built as water-storage facilities can be enormous, often taking the form of flooded land which provides many interesting features. Most reservoirs that offer game fishing are stocked with rainbow trout and brown trout throughout the year. Although the size of the venue frequently results in fish that become wild after spending many years in their environment. Natural lakes offer some of the most scenic fly-fishing available and often hold an indigenous fish population. Unfortunately, many anglers feel intimidated by the enormity of large venues and this often discourages them from trying their luck. The key to success is to break up the lake into manageable sections, thinking of each area as a smaller stillwater in its own right.

Lochs

In areas, such as Scotland and Ireland the term "loch" is used to describe a small stillwater. These venues are lakes to all intent and purposes, but they also possess some unique features that require classification. For example, Scottish hill lochs are set at high altitude and present the adventurous fly-fisher with the prospect of isolated sport in a complete wilderness environment. Irish lowland lochs are vast inland seas that provide habitat to many fish, including some specimen wild brown trout that attract anglers from around the world.

Fly-fishing from a boat is a great way to explore a large stillwater venue such as a Scottish loch.

It is well worth fishing near weed bed as they are home to many aquatic insects and fish in search of food.

STILLWATER FLY-FISHING WATER/FEATURES

Feeder streams and outlets

Water entering stillwater venues does so through feeder streams that provide a flow of oxygen and steady supply of food. Water flowing away from stillwaters is called an outlet and will also attract fish. These areas can be extremely productive during periods of hot weather, when the amount of dissolved oxygen in the water reduces. The movement provided by incoming and outgoing water allows fish to breath effectively for little effort as the water flows over their gills.

Drop off

Shelter is an important survival instinct. Fish seek their shelter in many areas, which depends on the environment in which they live, but frequently choose a drop off in stillwater. Drop offs are areas of land below the surface of the water that increase in gradient, sometimes suddenly, forming a ledge. Species such as trout feed happily on the shallow ledge in the knowledge that they may retreat to deep water if threatened. This feature attracts small fish that use the drop off to camouflage themselves from predators that frequently patrol the area looking for food. Aquatic insects also seek refuge in the material

that forms a drop off. As a result, an angler would be unwise to overlook this important feature.

Pinnacles of land offer a likely starting point, as do ditches, dams, hedges, old submerged roads and riverbeds. There is no need, however, to equip yourself with subaqua gear and actively search out these features! Instead seek local knowledge, look at contour maps of the land prior to flooding and observe the terrain around the venue for clues about what might lay below the surface of the water.

The same methods may not apply when fly-fishing from a boat, in reality the craft should be positioned near the shoreline and the features described will often be observed. Failing the presence of any obvious clues look directly into the water itself. Clear water, in particular, will offer an angler using Polaroid sunglasses the opportunity to view possible features, while areas of dark water next to light water may reveal the presence of a drop off.

Weed

Many forms of aquatic life, such as shrimps, thrive in subsurface weed and fish can regularly be observed patrolling these areas as they feed from the vegetation. Be ready for a hooked fish to dive into weed and where possible, try to prevent it from doing so.

Nonphysical features

A lot of evidence available to the observant fly-fisher may go unnoticed. For example, birds such as swallows and swifts, which fly close to the surface of the water, may seem like a welcome addition to a sunny lakeside environment. In fact, they will be feeding on hatching insects which, in turn, will be attracting the attention of hungry fish!

Areas of flat water among rippled sections are known as wind lanes and create a sticky surface tension on the stillwater. Hatching flies struggle to release themselves from wind lanes. This does not go unnoticed by the local fish population and it is quite amazing to find fish rising within a wind lane, seemingly in the middle of nowhere.

Finally, never be afraid to ask fellow fly-fishers or the fishery owner where the hot spots are. Most people, especially business owners who have a vested interest in getting anglers back to their venues, will be only too pleased to offer their assistance.

RIVER FLY-FISHING VENUES
Chalk streams

A meandering chalk stream is a trout angler's delight, but their popularity has resulted in some venues charging exorbitant permit fees to fish them. This is especially true for chalkstreams situated within striking distance of cities such as London. The alkaline water that flows along the length of a chalk stream is often called "gin clear", and it is this characteristic that provides superb opportunities to enjoy a visual fishing experience.

Percolating through porous rock, such as chalk, the mineral-rich water residing in underground aquifers is unable to permeate the clay riverbed characteristic of many chalk streams and begins its journey to the sea. The chemical and physical qualities of a chalkstream allow it to support abundant weed, insect and fish populations. Chalk streams are regarded as the birth place of fly-fishing, producing many famous anglers and works of literature during the sport's relatively short history.

Fly-fishing on a river is a peaceful, relaxing way to spend a few hours.

Spate rivers

Unlike their chalk stream cousins, spate rivers are fed by rain water that falls onto hills and then cascades down through a valley. The amount of precipitation determines the flow of water, which can reduce to a mere trickle in very dry conditions. Heavy rainfall will have an almost instant effect on a spate river, especially those found at the bottom of steep gorges. Prolonged downpours can lead to sharp rises in the water level. The fast-flowing current caused by this sudden increase in water volume is powerful and erodes soft banks, leading to high silt content during a spate. Water gushing off the hills also adds to the sediment and rapidly colours the water. The turbulent conditions are not favoured by resident fish, because they must exert energy to cope with the current. In addition, their ability to breathe is hampered by the muddy water. There is little point in fishing in these circumstances. However, the visibility will begin to return just after a spate and this can encourage fish to feed, providing a good opportunity to employ fly-fishing tactics. Spate rivers are favoured by migratory species such as salmon, which travel to spawning grounds in times of high water. This is a period of much excitement among anglers!

A beautiful dark pool on the famous River Lyn in north Devon.

Pools

The ability to read a river is vital to successful fly-fishing and requires knowledge of the terms used to describe the features present within each venue. A typical stretch of river is called a beat. It is made up of runs that denote sections of water with a fairly uniform width, followed by areas that widen, known as pools. A typical pool starts with a narrow section known as a throat — a prime position for large trout. After the throat comes the body, which is the main section of the pool and may contain a number of features, such as overhanging shelter, rocks and weed. The body may also be deep, offering shelter to the fish prior to narrowing into a rapid section of water, called the tail. Fishing in the tail will often be successful during the evening. However, it is the main body of the pool and the throat that offers the best chance of success. Look for pools on a beat map. These maps often feature named pools to help anglers identify their location.

Casting a pike fly into the margins on Chew Valley Lake in north Somerset.

Fly-fishing can be adapted to catch predators, such as this fine pike.

FLY-FISHING FOR PIKE
IN LAKES AND CANALS

In the past, huge pike flies, similar to Christmas decorations dangling from a fly rod, were met with a great deal of curiosity from fellow anglers. Times have changed, however and today the impressive lures required to pursue these exciting species are a familiar sight at many large trout venues, such as the famous Chew Valley Reservoir in north Somerset. Surviving on a mixed diet of resident coarse fish coupled with the high-protein qualities of stocked trout, pike found on these venues can attain impressive weights and offer the best chance of hooking a wild double figure fish in European waters.

Fly-fishing for pike on reservoirs is a lot of fun but requires a reasonable level of casting ability to cope with the air-resistant flies and distances necessary to be successful. Conversely canal venues are often relatively narrow, providing an ideal opportunity to practice the casts and tactics required to target pike. Many fly-caught canal pike are hooked at close range, resulting in spectacular sport that is particularly exciting on clearwater venues. Search for lakes and canals offering decent water clarity to provide the best chance of success and an opportunity to witness the fish taking the fly.

Features to look out for when fly-fishing for pike include many that also apply to trout, such as drop offs and in particular, weed beds. Fish preyed upon by pike seek refuge in these areas and therefore the predator will not be far away. Reed-lined banks are another favoured location. Don't ignore any artificial structures such as bridges and pontoons, which offer cover to many species of fish. When trying to locate pike, always give some thought to their food source and camouflage requirements.

Heading to the coast to cast a fly offers exciting sport in unrivalled surroundings.

A fly-caught bass is carefully released.

SALTWATER FLY-FISHING IN ESTUARIES AND ROCK MARKS

Fly-fishing for saltwater species such as bass has enjoyed a huge growth in popularity across coastal regions of Europe. These areas may also offer the possibility of connecting with a varied range of fish including garfish, mackerel and pollack. Predatory in nature, these species will follow schools of baitfish, such as sand eels and can be frequently seen attacking them at the surface of the water. Corralled together, the frightened ball of bait also attracts attention from above in the form of seabirds, which can be observed diving into the water to feed. This provides an important clue regarding the whereabouts of the target species and should be investigated immediately. Cast a fly into the commotion and it shouldn't take long for a hook up to transpire.

If seabirds do not reveal the presence of the target fish, then you will need to recognise underwater features that will attract the bait. For example, bass are frequently found in estuaries that provide a nursery ground to their prey, which includes crabs, shrimp and smaller fish. By contrast, pollack are a deep-water species and therefore a shoreline rock mark will be the best opportunity to capture this hard-fighting adversary. However, it is also possible to practice saltwater fly-fishing techniques from a boat or similar craft such as a kayak.

Fishing from a boat allows the use of specialist equipment to locate underwater features, such as drop offs and gullies. However, this is not possible when casting from the shore. Instead, you can investigate the chosen fishing ground at low tide to reveal the features that will be submerged during high tide. Fishing a rising tide is highly recommended, although it is extremely important to take the necessary safety precautions to prevent the possibility of falling into turbulent water or becoming cut off. Remain alert of this changing environment.

Extreme saltwater fly-fishing for coalfish off the coast of Norway.

FLY-FISHING TECHNIQUES

A good cast is more likely to catch a fish, so practice is the key to success.

Casting techniques for the fly-fisher seem to be unlike those used in coarse and sea fishing, but the basis of the cast is actually very similar.

Fly casting

In a process known as loading, the fly-fisher uses the weight of the fly line to bend the rod. This allows the blank to store energy which, upon straightening, transfers to the line. This results in momentum that allows the fly line to carry a leader and the fly toward the target. No matter how knowledgeable an angler may be regarding a venue, its features and the methods required to catch fish, it's all worthless without the ability to cast effectively.

Getting ready for casting

Time spent fly-fishing should be an enjoyable experience, so practising casts so that they become effortless is time well spent. The equipment should be balanced (see tackle section pages 80–95) and more importantly handled with a soft grip, which will allow the tackle to work effectively. Gripping your rod too tightly will cause vibrations within the blank, which appear in the line as waves. This leads to a lack of distance and accuracy, coupled with a splashy entrance into the water that will scare fish. To maintain a comfortable grip place your thumb on top of the handle and wrap the remaining fingers around it in the same way you would hold a screwdriver. Alternative grips exist, but the "thumb on top method" is by far the most popular and highly recommended.

A comfortable grip should be accompanied by relaxed shoulders, arm and wrist, although it will take practise to achieve this restful state while maintaining sufficient control during the cast. To further assist casting proficiency, a good foundation should be provided in the form of a suitable stance. There are two favoured methods of standing while casting: the close stance and the open stance.

The closed stance is achieved by standing with the toes pointing forward, with one foot slightly behind the other. Most anglers place the foot on the same side as the chosen casting arm in front — a method widely adopted by river anglers when accurate casts are required.

The open stance allows an angler to cast across the front of his or her body with feet set adjacent to one another and toes pointing sideways. Use an open stance in most circumstances and especially when making the elongated strokes required to execute distance casts.

Casting from a boat is far more comfortable and enjoyable if a commercially available seat is used to provide back support.

An angler demonstrates the majestic roll cast.

THE ULTIMATE GUIDE TO FISHING

The roll cast

One of the first skills for a newcomer to fly-fishing to master should be the roll cast. It will prove beneficial for many years to come. It is necessary to straighten the line prior to using alternative casting techniques, such as the overhead cast, because the line must be able to place tension upon the rod. The roll cast takes slack out of the line, which is particularly useful just after the rod has been threaded and the line placed on the water in readiness for the initial casts. This technique is also useful in areas surrounded by trees and as a method to surface sinking lines.

How to perform a roll cast

Once the rod has been threaded and the leader tied on, ensure that around two rod lengths of fly line are protruding from the rod tip. Place the line on the surface of the water. Follow the steps below, using the photographs opposite to guide you.

1) Assume a comfortable stance and grip (first finger trapping the line against the cork), with the tip of the rod positioned just above the water. This low starting point is important whatever casting technique you intend to use.
2) Using your elbow, gradually draw the rod backward and slide the line across the water, straightening it in the process. Once the movements are completed, the line should hang from the rod tip forming a "D" shape known as a D loop.
3) Apply power in the form of smooth acceleration generated from the elbow and with the aim of stopping the rod at 10am.
4) This controlled stop should send the line out over the water. As it straightens, smoothly lower the rod, returning to the original position.

Note: Practise the roll cast enough and you will be able to anchor the line with the opposite hand rather than using a finger to trap it against the cork.

Faults with roll casts

A lesson with a qualified instructor is the best way to learn, but you should be aware of some of the reasons for poor casting technique. First and foremost, never rush your roll cast. It's important to ensure a D Loop falls behind the rod. Do not accelerate with too much or too little force because this will be ineffective, resulting in poor presentation. The amount of power required to execute a successful cast takes practise but, as a guide, try to imagine the action of tapping a small nail into a wall when roll casting. Tangles appear more often if the rod tip crosses over the line as power is applied — a fault that is easily rectified by ensuring the D Loop is lined up with the target. Aim the rod straight down the line and allow the rod tip to stop well above the water or the line will not extend and will collapse into the water in the process.

The overhead cast

This is the most recognisable fly cast and is used in many situations when distance is required in wide open spaces. After straightening the line with a roll cast, an overhead cast employs a series of rhythmical strokes to create a shape within the line known as a loop. The ability to form a loop and understand how it works will improve your technique, resulting in consistently good presentations. The loop is formed when the rod comes to a stop and with practise, it is possible to control the size of this loop through varying the length of each stroke. Loops are either wide or narrow and both have significance at one time or another. Generally, it is worth practising narrow loops as this shape has very little wind resistance and an aerodynamic profile that will slice through the air effectively. The result is often a long, accurate cast (when coupled with good timing), although time should be spent with a qualified instructor to hone the skills required. There are also many handbooks and DVDs available to further assist your overhead casting technique.

1

2

4

5

How to perform an overhead cast

1) Start with the rod tip close to the surface of the water and trap the line against the cork with your first finger. This provides an anchor point and ensures that the line cannot slip up and down the rod in an uncontrolled manner. Ensure the line has no slack within it. Use a roll cast to straighten the line if necessary.

2) Start by lifting your rod tip smoothly, using your elbow and peeling the line from the surface of the water in the process.

3) As the rod tip reaches the 10am position (2pm for left-handed casters), accelerate swiftly aiming to stop the rod in a near vertical position. Novices should aim for the 1pm position (11am for a left-handed caster). Use your thumb to assist by allowing

3

but can be assisted by chanting "TICK" or "WAIT" as the line straightens out, although some anglers prefer to watch the lines progress.

5) The moment the line fully extends, accelerate smoothly forward to a 10am position (2pm for left-handed casters). Allow the line to unroll into the forward cast. Chant "TOCK" or "PUSH".

6) Allow the line to unroll into the forward cast.

Overhead casting – shooting line

Extending the line through the rod rings to reach your target is possible using a technique known as shooting. To increase the length, swap the finger used to trap line against the cork for the opposite hand. Grip the line firmly so that it does not slip through the hand in the middle of the cast. Each time the rod stops on the forward cast allow a little line to pass through the hand by gently releasing the pressure placed on it by the fingers. Novice anglers will need to practise this skill very carefully, allowing only a few inches of line to pass through the hand at any one time. Eventually, the amount of line shot can be increased. It is very important to realise that no more than three false casts — fewer if possible — are required to shoot adequate amounts of line. When using a weight forward line (see tackle pages 80–81), it is crucial that only the head section is extended beyond the rod tip. Shooting running line will result in a collapsed cast. To assist with releasing, which should only ever take place as the rod comes to a standstill, chant "TICK, TOCK, RELEASE". Add a brief pause between each word in the chant.

6

it to stop in an upright position just outside the eye. A distance of around 12in (30cm) between eye and thumb is correct.

4) To complete this movement, known as a back cast, allow the line to form a loop and straighten out completely. As the line unrolls and then straightens, it will place tension upon the rod, loading the blank in the process. Timing this exactly takes practice,

Faults with overhead casts

Casting faults can be many and varied but the same problems tend to occur consistently among individuals. With all types of casts, the most common mistake is an inability to control the wrist. Allowing the wrist to rock backward and forward with little or no control causes an elongated rod stroke that result in wide loops. The lack of aerodynamics within the line, which results from a wide loop, means that it is unable to extend properly and therefore will not bend the rod effectively. A broken wrist is also one of the main faults responsible for low back casts, which can be frustrating as the hook catches in obstructions and even the ground. To help cure a broken wrist, observe the thumb during the back cast and aim to stop in an upright position. This will prevent your wrist from bending backward. Forward wrist break can be avoided by ensuring the rod tip stops high,

rather than being forced toward the water. In this event, the line will crash down and cause a great amount of disturbance.

A lack of good timing will result in a loud snap sound, similar to the sound heard when cracking a whip. This problem can be cured by chanting to assist timing or by watching the line unfurl. It is important to cure poor timing because there are a number of unfortunate consequences associated with it, such as broken leaders and damaged fly lines. Poor timing will also prevent the line from straightening and the rod bending effectively, which is at the core of good fly casting techniques.

Tailing loops are another common fault within an overhead cast and have a number of causes, although the main culprit is applying power unevenly. Casting strokes should be as smooth as possible to avoid this error, which results in exasperating tangles in multiple fly rigs or loops in the leader that pull tight to form a wind knot. These knots must be cut out because they lower the breaking strain of the leader.

It's never wise to imitate a windmill, with arms flailing back and forth, when fly casting! Instead maintain a relaxed stance and comfortable grip, keeping your elbow in a relaxed position. Cast from the elbow using minimal wrist movement and never feel that adding force to the cast will help with distance. In fact, this usually has the opposite effect and results in a saying that applies to almost all cases of fly casting: "Less is more".

The side cast

When a loop extends during a regular overhead cast it does so in a vertical plane. This works very effectively over stillwaters, but if the intention is to pass the fly under an overhanging object, such as the branch of a tree, a standard overhead cast will result in a line snag. A side cast can be used to overcome this problem and the basic technique required is outlined as follows:

1) Pick up your rod as if you were going to make an overhead cast.
2) Turn your wrist so that the back of the hand faces the ground in a horizontal plane.
3) Adopt the same technique that you would use for the overhead cast.

During a side cast, the line will be positioned nearer the ground or water. As a result, it may be necessary to speed up the overall casting stroke. To practise a side cast for the first time, try performing an overhead cast and then steadily move the hand into a horizontal position while false casting. This gradual change in casting style will soon become second nature, allowing horizontal loops to be formed that will pass under obstacles.

Spey casting

Spey casting is one of the most famous methods of presenting a fly to a fish. It's a skill widely practised with two-handed rods by salmon anglers, but the technique can also be used with single-handed rods. Perhaps the most beautiful of all casting disciplines, the Spey cast is perceived to be complicated by many anglers, but in effect it is nothing more than a roll cast that incorporates a change of direction. The Spey cast takes its name from the famous Scottish river. The cast is used on venues that seldom allow a full overhead cast, due to the presence of trees or a high bank.

Once the cast has been made, the line is allowed to drift downstream with the current until it comes to rest to the point where the angler is situated. A series of movements is then made so the D Loop associated with roll casting can be placed in a position, in line with the target, on the opposite bank. There are many different types of Spey casts, including the single Spey, snap T and snake roll. Each one has a use that depends on the prevailing wind direction and whether the right or the left side of the river is to be fished.

Lengthy two-handed rods are often used when Spey casting to allow large amounts of line to be manoeuvred. These rods also prove useful when trying to control a salmon that's fighting hard in fast water. Getting to grips with these long rods, when Spey casting for the first time, should be done under the watchful eye of an instructor and only with a practised knowledge of roll casting. The following single Spey cast is not difficult to learn and is used on the bank of a river during an upstream wind.

How to perform a basic single Spey cast – double-handed rod

1) Start with the rod low to the water, with around two to three rod lengths of line protruding from the tip ring. If you are casting off the left bank (looking downstream), the right hand should be up the rod and the left hand down the rod. Your stance should reflect your hand position. Right hand up the rod, left foot forward and vice versa.

2) Smoothly lift the rod tip, gently peeling line from the water's surface and ensuring no slack develops. Start to sweep the rod tip across the body, rotating your hips in the process. The rod tip should dip very slightly. Imagine the shape of a smile to assist with the shallow dip that is required.

3) Continue rotating the hips. This process will eject the line from the water and place it on the right. Aim to create the D Loop of a roll cast, pausing to allow the line time to form the shape and begin loading the rod.

4) The moment the line has touched the water and created a large D Loop, drive the rod tip forward smoothly, using the bottom hand to pull the rod butt into the body. Stop the rod tip high to allow a loop to form and release any slack line available, shooting it into the forward cast.

Note: The single Spey is just one of a number of different casts within this group. You will need to learn each cast depending on the bank to be fished and wind direction. You will also need to change hands depending on the wind direction and the bank you intend to fish.

1

2

3

4

Faults with Spey casting

Most Spey casting mistakes develop because anglers rush the cast and in particular, they do not allow the line to straighten correctly. Make sure that the line is taut and positioned downstream prior to commencing the required movements. Dipping the rod tip during the cast – rather than following a horizontal plane – is another mistake that forces the line into the water, making it difficult to release from the surface tension. The result is a cast that will collapse.

Bad timing is a common cause of ineffective Spey casts. Since the D Loop will not develop correctly,

once again this results in poor tensioning of the rod. However, waiting too long will produce a negative effect as the line will become stuck in the water and is difficult to release. A familiar Spey casting mistake, made by trout fishers moving into salmon fishing with double-handed rods, is to push with the top hand which sends the rod tip toward the water and with it the line.

Correcting a number of errors can be tricky, so it is wise to work on each stage of the cast as a separate element and then piece each part together. This process can be accelerated by videoing casting technique prior to analysis.

FLY-FISHING TACTICS

It is important to locate the feeding depth of the trout, especially in deep-water venues such as Clatworthy in Somerset.

Time has helped to evolve a myriad of stillwater fly-fishing tactics and techniques all designed to get the better of our chosen species.

STILLWATER FLY-FISHING FOR TROUT

As wily as fish may seem at some times, the reality is that they are just fish! Our tactics must be adopted to suit the conditions that present themselves. This is a huge subject that can be broken down into several different criterias. More often than not, it is the simple methods that prove to be successful time and time again. Overcomplicating matters may lead an angler into the trap of pondering over flies for too long or moving position too regularly. This is wasted energy. If the fly is not in the water we won't catch any fish.

STILLWATER FLY-FISHING FOR TROUT — WET-FLY TACTICS

Finding depth and retrieving

During periods of cold weather, trout will frequently feed on bloodworm — the larva of the buzzer pupa — at the depths of the river.

Use an appropriate artificial fly and present it near the bottom of the lake on a sinking line. To work out the rough depth at which the fish are residing, it is important to count down a sinking line (or leader) as it descends. By systematically performing this ritual on every cast, it will be possible to recognise the position at which the fish are feeding. Takes may occur in a variety of ways, although a firm tug on the line detected by a finger is the most obvious sign. The first finger of the rod hand is used to trap the fly line gently against the underneath of the cork handle of the rod, while the opposite hand is used to pull the fly line back through the rings, adding life to the fly. This technique is known as "retrieving" and is designed to provoke a fish into devouring the artificial pattern. A well-chosen retrieve is perhaps one of the most important fly-fishing skills to master.

Fishing with buzzers

Many variations of artificial buzzer pupae are available, but a plain black version incorporating eye-catching triggers, such as a bright wing bud, is hard to beat.

This very versatile pattern can be fished on a variety of lines throughout the year on small and large stillwaters. A common retrieve used when fishing with buzzers and that other great suggestive pattern, the Diawl Bach, is accomplished by forming small loops of line within the palm of the hand. The technique, known as the "figure-eight" (owing to the shape produced in the line as it is retrieved), is very adaptable and can be used in conjunction with a wide range of tactics.

The slim profile of these Epoxy Buzzers enables them to sink quickly to the depth required.

A reliable set of flies (from left): Orange Blob, Holographic Red Cormorant, Silver Stealth Buzzer, Cormorant Booby and Flashback Damsel.

The dead drift

Retrieving is not the only way of presenting artificial fly patterns in a realistic manner. The affect of wind drift upon a fly line will also provide additional action. Cast across a breeze blowing on the noncasting shoulder and allow the flies to drift with the current.

The washing line

To suspend flies naturally in the water column, construct a leader that incorporates droppers and attach these to patterns such as the Diawl Bach. Complete the arrangement by tying a booby in the point fly position.

This tactic, known as the washing line, suspends a string of flies naturally and the sink rate can be controlled by varying the size of the booby eyes and therefore the overall buoyancy.

Indicator fishing

A successful method of locating depth is to use a sight indicator that acts in the same way as a coarse angler's float. Easily viewed from a distance, you can fish a number of flies below an indicator as a team, spacing the patterns at intervals throughout the leader to cover a range of depth. This tactic works well with buzzers. Take the register as a submerged indicator, which requires a strike to hook the fish.

Lure fishing

There are many varieties of lure available, including the now-infamous Blob. Fished at high speed with a strip retrieve taking the form of long pulls, these gaudy patterns attract the attention of newly introduced stock fish, although resident specimens are also susceptible. It is worth noting that a rapid retrieve is not always necessary.

Fishing with indicators is exciting and often successful.

Strip retrieving a fly line into a line tray.

Teams of flies

A multiple fly rig provides a good opportunity to experiment with size and shade of fly. The most popular methods incorporate both lures and imitative flies into a team — the attractor fly draws the attention of the fishes to more subtle lifelike patterns.

Stalking tactics

This is a popular method of fishing that is regularly practised on small stillwaters with heavy flies known as stalking bugs. A roving heronlike approach is best adopted when stalking, using cover wherever available and a set of Polaroid glasses to spot the fish.

Once a fish is located, aim a cast so that the heavily weighted stalking bug falls well in front of the cruising target. As the fish nears, commence a retrieve to animate the fly or gently raise the rod to lift it through the water column enticingly in front of the fish.

Colourful stalking bugs sink quickly to depth and incorporate several important features, such as a mobile tail.

STILLWATER FLY-FISHING FOR TROUT – DRY-FLY TACTICS

There are few things in fly-fishing more revered than the opportunity to fish with a dry fly. Waiting expectantly in the hope that at any moment a well-presented surface pattern will be devoured is the stuff of fly-fishing dreams. An exciting visual method, dry fly-fishing is a relatively simple tactic that can be applied to a wide range of stillwater and moving-water venues.

Applying floatant to dry flies

Do not swamp flies with floatant. Instead, melt a little between a couple of fingers before massaging into the body and hackle.

Melt a gel floatant, such as Gherkes Gink, between your fingers prior to applying it to a dry fly.

It is very important to degrease the leader with a sinking paste or liquid when fishing with dry flies.

Dry-fly presentation

The simplest way of dry fly-fishing requires just one buoyant pattern, such as a Hopper or Big Black, to be attached to a tapered copolymer leader.

Prior to casting, the fly must be treated with a floatant and then the leader degreased with a sinking agent so that it descends below the surface. Fish that intercept the fly with a swirl, without taking the fly, have often been spooked by a floating leader, so the time spent perfecting presentation is well worth the effort. A successful presentation will result in a confident reaction as the fish breaks the surface of the water to accept the fly, requiring a firm lift of the rod to set the hook.

Teams of dry flies

Fishing with a single dry fly does work and is perfect for beginners, but it provides just one chance of catching a fish. Another distinct disadvantage is that the target fish must be travelling almost in line with the fly if it is to see it. A team of flies can be employed to increase the odds of catching a fish on a dry fly. This approach has many advantages, which include the ability to alter size, colour and variety of fly throughout the leader. In addition, a selection of patterns can be cast across the path of a trout. Flies presented as a profile across the fish increase the chances of them being seen from many angles.

Fishing dry flies blind

Many anglers assume that fish must be witnessed rising before a dry fly approach should be adopted, but this is not always the case – it is possible to tempt unsighted fish. Clear water fisheries provide trout with a decent view of the surface and therefore flies incorporating a strong silhouette may entice them from the depths to take.

Poised with a net, this angler has stopped fishing to land a fish for his boat partner.

Boat fishing

The ability to move rapidly from one area to the next is an advantage to be enjoyed when going afloat with fly-fishing tactics. It's also possible to cover a greater range of depths from a boat, while features such as wind lanes are placed within easy reach. A comfortable day on the water is assisted by the use of quality boat seats that incorporate a back rest. A net with a long handle also help to land fish. Drifting under the power of the wind and current can be very productive, because it is possible to cover large expanses of water.

A drogue, which is essentially an underwater parachute, must be used to slow the boat and control the drift. Safety is important whenever spending time near water but especially when boat fishing. Always wear a buoyancy aid and where possible, do not go afloat alone. Plenty of provisions, a first-aid kit and communications devices are essential items to pack.

River fly-fishing for trout and grayling

Picture a fly-fishing scene. Most people would describe a beautiful river, with an angler situated midflow, carefully casting a fly to the unsuspecting fish. This serene image is far from a dream but readily available throughout Europe. The fish may be smaller than those found on stocked stillwaters, but there is every likelihood that they are wild. The opportunity to catch indigenous species in wondrous places is the attraction of river fishing. Fly-fishing on rivers is also far from difficult if casting and good presentation is practised. Find fish on rivers by looking for their presence based on the fundamental requirements of survival – food, shelter and oxygen.

RIVER FLY-FISHING FOR TROUT AND GRAYLING – WET-FLY TACTICS

Downstream and across

The simplest river fishing tactic requires a fly to be presented across stream that swings with the current. In broken water this can prove to be a successful technique, but it is not recommended on flat water or deep pools. Flies that would be appropriate include nymphs and spider patterns. Spiders are characterised by a sparse body and soft hackle that represents a fly that has drowned and has been caught below the water's surface as it attempted to hatch.

New Zealand dropper

This is a famous tactic that has proved to be controversial, resulting in a ban on some venues. Chalk stream venues in particular are often opposed to the New Zealand dropper, so fishery rules should be confirmed before using it. The New Zealand dropper incorporates a dry fly as a sight indicator situated on a dropper, with a nymph suspended below. If the buoyant pattern disappears, a swift raise of the rod may result in a hooked fish. Some takes will be false alarms if the nymph has snagged a rock or similar obstruction, but many will result in success. The New Zealand dropper is best fished up stream to retain perfect control.

Czech nymph

The Czech nymph was developed as a way of fishing close to the riverbed with patterns that represent caddis. The standard method requires the presentation of three flies slightly upstream, providing enough time for the patterns to sink. A long rod assists as the fly line should barely touch the water, allowing a natural presentation unhindered by the drag of the current acting upon it.

Carry several copies of each artificial fly pattern such as these Czech nymphs in case any are lost while fishing.

Upstream nymph

The upstream nymph is one of the most difficult techniques to practise, but the effort and high level of concentration is well worth it, resulting in a natural presentation. Cast a nymph upstream and allow it to sink while retrieving exactly in time with the flow and then raise the rod tip smoothly at the end of the drift to lift the fly up in the water layers. A positive response is seen as a twitch on the line, which requires a swift strike or as a fish hooking itself on the fly as it ascends.

RIVER FLY-FISHING FOR TROUT AND GRAYLING – DRY-FLY TACTICS

Upstream dry fly

Despite the many tactics available to the adaptable fly-fisher, the upstream dry-fly method is both highly enjoyable and relatively simple. Furthermore, on some venues, specifically chalk streams in southern England, it is the only method allowed. To determine the choice of fly, observe the water for signs of insects being consumed, paying close attention to the colour and size of any insects seen, because this will help to match the artificial fly to the hatch. In some instances, the fish become so selective that the artificial will need to be a close copy of their natural food or they will refuse to take.

Fishing upstream with dry flies has been adapted to the trout and grayling habit of sitting with their heads facing into the current, enabling them to enjoy optimum oxygen and food benefits for very little effort. To mimic the path of their surface food, a dry fly is cast so that it lands well in front of the fish, giving it plenty of time to see

Casting an artificial nymph or dry fly upstream offers a natural presentation.

the fly. The leader should pass over the fish's back and the fly line is positioned well behind the tail. Practise accurate casting and these requirements will soon become second nature. After a cast is made, it is very important to retrieve the fly in time with the flow of water without allowing it to drag. Drag is a disturbance caused by the fly as it moves faster than the current and should be avoided.

Salmon and sea trout tactics

Imitating a fish's diet calls for a repertoire of techniques to cope with the different conditions. However, most migratory fish that enter European waters, such as salmon and sea trout, do so to spawn, not to feed. This means that the most effective approach to adopt when trying to capture migratory species is to produce an aggressive reaction through the attractive qualities of a lure.

Salmon fishing is best practised after rainfall has resulted in a rise in water levels, followed by a steady fall, an event that inspires the fish to move upstream. This occurrence is known as a run of fish and can take place throughout the year, largely depending on geographical location or weather conditions. The key runs of fish happen in the late spring and autumn, which is the period of time that most salmon anglers concentrate their efforts.

Salmon flies are wonderful creations, but it is hard to beat the Stoat's Tail series of flies or Cascades. Carry a variety of sizes and colour combinations, using the darker flies in clear water and adopting the brighter flies when there is less clarity. Salmon are often located in areas where they can gain high levels of oxygen or enjoy some rest after working through a fast run or pool.

Salmon fishing techniques are relatively simple. Cast a fly across stream so that it swings through likely fish-holding features and wait in anticipation of a take. A hooked fish frequently registers as a heavy feeling on the line. Do not lift suddenly! Instead, gently raise the rod and allow the line to tighten up against the reel.

Sea trout are approached in a similar manner to salmon although the fly colour is less important. Fishing at night is a proven tactic with sunk lures incorporating a strong silhouette. Floating, sink tip and intermediate lines offer a range of prospects, but daytime fishing in high water with a sunken line and fly intended for salmon frequently results in a sea trout. This enigmatic species will also take surface flies, such as the Chernobyl Ant, fished on a warm evening under an overcast sky. Ensure that darkness has fallen prior to fishing and learn the venue to be fished by, observing it through the day, although sea trout pools should not be disturbed for several hours prior to fishing. A head torch will be required to tie flies, but under no circumstances shine the light into the water as this will ruin the fishing. Fly-fishing at night for sea trout is one of the most difficult forms of the sport, but it is incredibly exciting when a fish is hooked and charging around a pool unseen.

This silver Stoat's Tail is a great salmon fly, especially in clear water.

Tempt salmon with a Cascade when the water is retaining colour after rainfall.

FAR LEFT : *Many salmon rivers are set in awe-inspiring scenery.*

Alternative fly-fishing tactics

Each species of fish opens up a whole new world of opportunity for the adaptable fly-fisher willing to try some alternative fishing. Fishing for sea bass with fly tactics is one example of this progress, increasing in popularity throughout Europe.

Saltwater fly-fishing can be enjoyed with very little tackle and flies such as the Clouser Minnow are frequently successful. Sea bass can be found in many estuaries and a rising tide presents a very good opportunity to target these and many other saltwater species, such as pollack.

Carp and pike are highly respected by coarse anglers, due to both their size and fighting ability. These powerful fish represent a serious opponent to fly-fishers and a great chance of taking a double figure fish on ultralightweight tackle. Pike flies such as the Bunny Bug are designed to resemble baitfish and should be cast in conjunction with a wire bite guard to protect against the pike's impressive dentures.

Many carp have been weaned onto pellet baits such as dog biscuits during their lives in a commercial coarse fishery – dog biscuit flies fashioned from deer hair fibres are the best approach! In some circumstances, carp will be seen to take natural flies such as daddy longlegs or mayflies off the surface, in which case an appropriate representation may provoke a response.

Playing fish with fly-fishing tackle

Although fly-fishing tackle is much lighter than many forms of coarse- and sea-fishing equipment, it is still equipped to deal with hard-fighting fish.

Follow these steps:

1. When a fish is hooked, keep the rod tip reasonably high. Do not raise it to a vertical point, however, because this could break the tip and will not place pressure on the fish.
2. If the fish runs, it is important to use the finger trapping the line underneath the cork handle as a brake. When the fish dives, release pressure gently allowing the line to skip over the finger. When it slows, reapply pressure with the finger and retrieve line with the opposite hand.
3. Be ready for a fish running back toward the shoreline or boat after being hooked and respond by pulling in line very quickly. Large hard-fighting fish should be played off the reel (set the drag to apply further pressure), because coils of line lying near obstacles could lead to a lost fish. Further braking can be applied by gently feathering the rotating spool with a hand.
4. If the hooked fish is to be released, play it hard and fast using a technique known as side strain to manoeuvre the fish away from snags. This is achieved by dropping the rod to a horizontal angle and then pulling to the side, in the opposite direction to the route chosen by the fish.
5. Always be alert through the fight but especially at the beginning, during powerful runs and toward the end when there may be a last bid for freedom, resulting in a sudden dive.
6. When the fish is beaten it will wallow on its side. Draw the rod over a shoulder steadily to slide the fish across the top of a net sunk well below the surface of the water.

OPPOSITE: *A landing net with a long handle helps to land a rainbow trout caught on a reservoir in Somerset.*

Sea Fishing

WELCOME TO SEA ANGLING

More and more anglers are discovering the excitement of sea angling – fishing either from boats or from the shore. Whether it's from a pier, rock, beach, private or charter boat, lots of anglers find themselves hooked by the allure of the freedom of the sea and by the sheer size of the fish that can be caught from under the surface waters of this natural environment.

Sea fishing has something for everyone. Some angler's sea fish for peace and quiet, others fish for food, while many others fish for the adrenalin rush of what they may catch – nature's lucky dip. Then, like the other disciplines of angling, some sea anglers fish competitively.

The main differences between coarse, fly and sea fishing, aside from the different tackle needed, boils down to three things. As yet in Britain, recreational sea anglers do not require a license or a fishery permit to fish. This makes sea fishing always available 24 hours a day and easy on the pocket. The second and most important difference, is that sea fish are not constrained to the lengths of a river or by the sides of a lake or loch. This means a sea angler has the added challenge of locating fish over a vast expanse of water before he can cast a bait for them. The final thing is that all sea anglers have an added natural element to deal with as well as weather-tides!

With sea fish being so delectable, it may come as no surprise that the roots of British and Irish recreational sea fishing were once deeply entwined in food-source fishing, but today this is not the case. Modern tackle, gadgets and computer-brained equipment, such as fish-finders and GPS navigation systems,

have pushed British sea angling into the 21st century and this is good for the sport.

Conservation is now paramount and most anglers only take what fish they require for the table, returning the rest to swim free. All anglers are now aware of size limits and many sea anglers set their own limits way above these to ensure there is still good sport for generations to come. Various bodies collect statistics and, with the recreational sea angler or RSA, now regarded as an important contributor to costal economy, sea anglers now have a voice alongside commercial fishing. This will help shape the sport into the future, and may it be a long future, now.

It is said that variety is the spice of life. Although you may specialise in catching certain types of sea fish, many anglers enjoy the variety that abounds beneath the surface of the sea and the different challenges in catching each species. One thing all sea angers share is the excitement of exploring new places and new marks to fish – offshore, inshore and from the coast – of which there is enough to last a lifetime and more.

The Greek word "pelagos" is roughly translated as "vast expanse of open water", and sums up our seas better than any other word. Whereas my fellow coarse and game authors, John and Nick, may be able to direct you to a piece of water and tell you what dwells there, with sea angling I can only point you in the right direction. The rest will be for you to find out as you explore! Hopefully by the time you finish reading this section of the book, you'll have enough knowledge to get out there on the water and start your own journey in sea fishing.

WEATHER AND TIDES

For the sea angler, weather and tidal conditions are not just a matter of comfort, but one of safety.

All coarse, fly and sea anglers have to deal with weather, but for the sea angler, it becomes a matter of safety as well as comfort. Tides can often dictate good or poor fishing but, like weather, they have certain factors that are important for all sea anglers to consider for their own safety. One moment it can be flat calm and sunny, but the next it can be overcast, squally and with rapidly building seas. It's extremely important for every sea angler to have a basic understanding of weather and tides. As the old saying goes "time and tide wait for no man", and nor does the weather.

Perfect surf-fishing conditions. Both the weather and the tides have a great influence over where to fish and which species to target.

Both weather and tides also have a great influence over the quality of fishing. The saying *"When the wind is from the east, the fish bite the least! And when the wind is from the west, the fish bite the best!"* is not just an empty phrase — it's very true! It will pay any sea angler dividends to learn both weather and tides for their own safety and to be able to understand and predict good fishing around any given conditions.

WEATHER

All sea fishing trips from shore and afloat are determined by the weather. Every sea angler should ask questions such as "Is it safe to go fishing?" and "Where would be the best place to go fishing?" in the days before a trip. Keep an eye on the weather in the days leading up to a trip so you can watch the movements of weather systems and form an idea of what is developing in advance. A basic knowledge of weather is needed to enable you to decipher the Meteorological Office synoptic charts and make your own forecast. Understanding the weather forecast will help you judge, in advance, if you're fishing or not and how to dress if you are. Knowing what the sea conditions could be will also let you choose which type fishing may be more productive.

High and low pressure weather systems

Basic weather is quite simple. There are two types of weather — good weather and bad weather. Good weather would include clear skies, light winds and good visibility. Bad weather would include rain, strong winds and poor visibility. Both good and bad weather are caused by different weather systems. Good weather is usually associated with high pressure systems and bad weather is usually associated with low-pressure systems. In general, if you have high pressure above your area, then you can expect good weather. If you have low pressure above your area — expect the opposite.

High-pressure systems and the associated "good weather" often develop to the south of Britain and move toward us in a northerly direction. In the northern hemisphere, winds rotate clockwise around a high pressure system.

Low-pressure systems and the associated "bad weather" are often born thousands of miles out in the Atlantic in an area called the Polar Front. This region is where polar winds from the north meet tropical winds from the south and rotate around each other, creating a low-pressure weather system. In the northern hemisphere, winds rotate counterclockwise around a low-pressure system.

Weather fronts

Fronts are areas on low-pressure systems where polar (cold) and tropical (warm) weather meet. These are often represented on weather charts as lines with semicircular or triangular symbols. On one side of these symbols is warm air and on the other is cold air. Fronts are usually where any bad weather will be felt including low cloud, rain, poor visibility and strengthening winds. High pressure systems don't have fronts.

Learning how to read synoptic charts (weather maps) will keep you safe and will also help you predict better fishing in the given conditions.

Warm fronts (red lines with semicircles on weather charts) are created by warm air rising. As a warm front approaches, the cloud thickens and lowers, the wind steadily increases and it will almost certainly rain.

Cold fronts (blue lines with triangles on weather charts) are created by fast, cold air falling. As a cold front approaches, it can be stormy with cloud and rain and winds increase. The skies quickly clear after the front has passed, but winds can remain strong and gusty for some time.

Occluded fronts (purple lines with semicircles and triangles on weather charts) are where cold weather has caught up with warm weather in the system. They are similar to warm fronts with low cloud and an increase in wind and rain. Occluded fronts often have lower wind speeds, but they can produce heavy downpours that last for hours.

Troughs (thick black lines on weather charts) are bands of cloud across the flow of the wind. Troughs are similar to cold fronts with heavy rain and squally strong winds. The weather from troughs is short-lived but extremely unpleasant.

Isobars and winds

All weather systems are drawn as circular rings, which look like a halved onion on weather charts. It is these rings that tell us how strong the winds will be. These lines are called isobars.

When the isobars are close together, this indicates strong winds. When they are well spaced, expect lighter winds. Don't expect close isobars to develop around low-pressure systems only. High-pressure systems can also have strong winds. All winds increase as a weather front approaches and they can be quite strong as it passes. Wind can be measured in miles per hour (mph) but are also measured as Force, from one to twelve, on the Beaufort scale, corresponding to speeds in knots. The Beaufort scale is mainly used by marine forecasters.

This angler has carefully considered the weather and tides and knows how far to push the conditions before it becomes unsafe.

FORCE	WIND SPEED	SEA STATE
1	1-3 knots (light)	ripples
2	4-6 knots (light breeze)	small wavelets
3	7-10 knots (gentle breeze)	occasional crests
4	11-16 knots (moderate breeze)	white horses
5	17-21 knots (fresh breeze)	moderate waves
6	22-27 knots (strong breeze)	large waves
7	28-33 knots (near gale)	breaking waves
8	34-40 knots (gale)	moderately high breaking waves
9	41-47 knots (severe gale)	high breaking waves
10	48-55 knots (storm)	very high breaking waves
11	56-63 knots (violent storm)	exceptionally high seas
12	over 64 knots (hurricane)	exceptionally high seas

Every sea angler needs to understand low- pressure systems and the associated fronts and winds to ensure safety and comfort while fishing. A coast with an offshore wind will be lovely and calm. A coast with a strong onshore breeze will be turbulent and possibly dangerous. An area where the wind and tide strongly oppose could be a lethal combination. Studying weather in further depth will not only make you safer but also help you catch more. A number of weather sources are available, including weather reports on local television and radio. However, the internet is now the best source of weather prediction for every sea angler.

At low tide these rocks in the Channel Islands are exposed. At high water, six hours later, they will be completely covered.

TIDES

There are two important reasons for understanding the tides, too. First, there's the safety/planning side of knowing your tides. Every sea angler should ask questions such as "is there enough water?" and "What will be the effects of the weather with the tides?" before heading out on a fishing expedition. Second, the tides are very influential to certain types of fishing and fish species. Tides play a big part in the day-to-day activities of every sea angler and a good understanding of them is needed to keep safe and catch fish. Tides are localised and their strengths and maximum heights vary from one coast to the next. To get to grips with tides, their differences and abnormalities, it will take time and further study of your own local area or the coast from which you intend to fish.

A word of warning. When strong winds and tides oppose, steep breaking seas can build quickly. This is often referred to as "wind against" or "across tide". In areas such as tidal races, where strong tides run, this wind against tide can be a lethal combination.

Tide times and local adjustments

Daily tidal information is available from a variety of sources, but the simplest way to find out what the tide is doing is to purchase a set of tide times

TIME ZONE (UT) For Summer Time add ONE hour in non-shaded areas	DOVER LAT 51°07'N LONG 1°19'E TIMES AND HEIGHTS OF HIGH AND LOW WATERS	Dates in red are SPRINGS Dates in blue are NEAPS YEAR 20

JANUARY

Time m	Time m
1 0333 1.7 / M 0859 6.1 / 1614 1.5 / 2134 6.0	**16** 0332 2.1 / TU 0845 5.6 / 1559 1.8 / 2119 5.7
2 0441 1.5 / TU 0956 6.2 / 1719 1.4 / 2225 6.1	**17** 0428 1.8 / W 0935 5.9 / 1652 1.5 / 2204 6.0
3 0539 1.3 / W 1047 6.3 / 1812 1.3 / 2309 6.4	**18** 0518 1.5 / TH 1020 6.1 / 1741 1.3 / 2245 6.3
4 0630 1.2 / TH 1132 6.4 / 1858 1.4 / 2351 6.5	**19** 0606 1.2 / F 1103 6.4 / 1829 1.2 / 2326 6.5
5 0717 1.2 / F 1213 6.3 / 1939 1.3	**20** 0653 1.0 / SA 1145 6.5 / 1915 1.1
6 0031 6.5 / SA 0758 1.2 / 1252 6.3 / 2015 1.4	**21** 0006 6.7 / SU 0739 0.9 / 1227 6.6 / 1958 1.0
7 0110 6.5 / SU 0836 1.2 / 1330 6.1 / 2048 1.5	**22** 0048 6.8 / M 0824 0.8 / 1308 6.6 / 2039 1.0
8 0148 6.4 / M 0910 1.3 / 1408 6.0 / 2116 1.6	**23** 0130 6.8 / TU 0906 0.8 / 1351 6.5 / 2118 1.0
9 0225 6.2 / TU 0940 1.5 / 1445 5.8 / 2143 1.7	**24** 0215 6.8 / W 0947 0.8 / 1437 6.4 / 2158 1.1
10 0300 6.0 / W 1011 1.6 / 1525 5.6 / 2216 1.9	**25** 0302 6.6 / TH 1028 1.0 / 1528 6.1 / 2241 1.4
11 0339 5.8 / TH 1048 1.8 / 1611 5.3 / 2257 2.1	**26** 0354 6.3 / F 1115 1.4 / 1627 5.8 / 2331 1.7
12 0426 5.5 / F 1135 2.0 / 1712 5.2 / 2350 2.3	**27** 0455 6.0 / SA 1211 1.7 / 1740 5.6
13 0530 5.3 / SA 1236 2.2 / 1824 5.1	**28** 0035 2.0 / SU 0611 5.6 / 1320 2.0 / 1903 5.6
14 0104 2.4 / SU 0642 5.2 / 1349 2.4 / 1930 5.2	**29** 0152 2.0 / M 0737 5.5 / 1437 2.1 / 2023 5.4
15 0225 2.4 / M 0748 5.4 / 1458 2.0 / 2028 5.4	**30** 0314 2.0 / TU 0858 5.6 / 1607 1.9 / 2132 5.7
	31 0436 1.7 / W 1003 5.9 / 1721 1.6 / 2223 6.0

FEBRUARY

Time m	Time m
1 0539 1.4 / TH 1051 6.1 / 1813 1.4 / 2304 6.3	**16** 0459 1.4 / F 1007 6.2 / 1725 1.3 / 2229 6.4
2 0629 1.2 / F 1130 6.2 / 1855 1.2 / 2341 6.5	**17** 0551 1.0 / SA 1050 6.5 / 1816 1.0 / 2310 6.7
3 0712 1.0 / SA 1204 6.3 / 1931 1.2	**18** 0641 0.8 / SU 1131 6.7 / 1903 0.8 / 2350 6.8
4 0017 6.6 / SU 0747 1.0 / 1237 6.3 / 2000 1.2	**19** 0729 0.5 / M 1210 6.8 / 1946 0.7
5 0051 6.6 / M 0818 1.0 / 1308 6.2 / 2025 1.2	**20** 0029 7.1 / TU 0811 0.4 / 1249 6.8 / 2023 0.6
6 0123 6.5 / TU 0842 1.1 / 1337 6.1 / 2045 1.3	**21** 0110 7.1 / W 0849 0.4 / 1330 6.8 / 2059 0.7
7 0150 6.4 / W 0905 1.2 / 1403 6.0 / 2109 1.4	**22** 0152 7.0 / TH 0905 0.7 / 1413 6.6 / 2135 0.9
8 0214 6.2 / TH 0931 1.4 / 1427 5.9 / 2137 1.6	**23** 0236 6.7 / F 1003 0.9 / 1500 6.2 / 2215 1.2
9 0240 6.0 / F 1002 1.6 / 1455 5.7 / 2211 1.8	**24** 0325 6.3 / SA 1046 1.4 / 1556 5.8 / 2302 1.7
10 0316 5.8 / SA 1039 1.9 / 1535 5.4 / 2253 2.1	**25** 0426 5.8 / SU 1140 1.9 / 1708 5.3
11 0405 5.4 / SU 1128 2.2 / 1637 5.0 / 2351 2.4	**26** 0006 2.1 / M 0545 5.3 / 1255 2.3 / 1838 5.1
12 0537 5.1 / M 1248 2.4 / 1846 4.9	**27** 0133 2.4 / TU 0730 5.2 / 1425 2.3 / 2017 5.2
13 0133 2.5 / TU 0715 5.1 / 1423 2.4 / 2000 5.2	**28** 0310 2.2 / W 0905 5.4 / 1614 2.0 / 2128 5.6
14 0300 2.2 / W 0824 5.4 / 1533 2.0 / 2058 5.6	
15 0401 1.8 / TH 0920 5.8 / 1632 1.6 / 2146 6.0	

MARCH

Time m	Time m
1 0440 1.7 / TH 1002 5.8 / 1716 1.6 / 2214 6.0	**16** 0337 1.7 / F 0900 5.8 / 1608 1.6 / 2123 6.1
2 0535 1.3 / F 1043 6.1 / 1801 1.3 / 2250 6.3	**17** 0434 1.3 / SA 0948 6.3 / 1702 1.2 / 2207 6.5
3 0619 1.0 / SA 1116 6.2 / 1839 1.1 / 2324 6.5	**18** 0529 0.9 / SU 1030 6.6 / 1754 0.9 / 2248 6.8
4 0656 0.9 / SU 1145 6.3 / 1910 1.1 / 2356 6.6	**19** 0621 0.6 / M 1110 6.8 / 1841 0.6 / 2327 7.1
5 0726 0.9 / M 1213 6.3 / 1935 1.1	**20** 0708 0.4 / TU 1148 6.9 / 1923 0.5
6 0027 6.6 / TU 0749 1.0 / 1241 6.3 / 1954 1.1	**21** 0007 7.2 / W 0749 0.3 / 1227 6.9 / 2000 0.5
7 0054 6.5 / W 0809 1.0 / 1305 6.3 / 2013 1.1	**22** 0048 7.2 / TH 0827 0.4 / 1308 6.8 / 2036 0.6
8 0115 6.4 / TH 0830 1.1 / 1324 6.2 / 2037 1.2	**23** 0129 7.0 / F 0902 0.6 / 1351 6.6 / 2113 0.8
9 0133 6.3 / F 0855 1.2 / 1343 6.1 / 2105 1.4	**24** 0214 6.7 / SA 0940 1.0 / 1439 6.2 / 2153 1.3
10 0158 6.0 / SA 0925 1.5 / 1412 6.0 / 2137 1.7	**25** 0304 6.2 / SU 1022 1.5 / 1536 5.7 / 2242 1.8
11 0232 5.9 / SU 0959 1.8 / 1451 5.7 / 2215 2.0	**26** 0407 5.6 / M 1118 2.1 / 1646 5.3 / 2350 2.4
12 0316 5.5 / M 1044 2.1 / 1542 5.4 / 2308 2.4	**27** 0528 5.1 / TU 1240 2.5 / 1814 5.0
13 0427 5.0 / TU 1151 2.5 / 1805 4.9	**28** 0123 2.4 / W 0727 5.1 / 1418 2.4 / 2000 5.2
14 0044 2.6 / W 0650 5.0 / 1351 2.4 / 1931 5.1	**29** 0305 2.1 / TH 0853 5.4 / 1551 2.0 / 2105 5.6
15 0230 2.3 / TH 0803 5.4 / 1508 2.0 / 2033 5.6	**30** 0420 1.7 / F 0941 5.7 / 1647 1.6 / 2148 6.0
	31 0510 1.3 / SA 1018 6.1 / 1731 1.3 / 2224 6.3

APRIL

Time m	Time m
1 0551 1.0 / SU 1048 6.2 / 1807 1.2 / 2257 6.4	**16** 0500 0.8 / M 1004 6.5 / 1723 0.9 / 2221 6.9
2 0625 1.0 / M 1117 6.3 / 1837 1.1 / 2329 6.5	**17** 0554 0.5 / TU 1045 6.7 / 1812 0.7 / 2303 7.1
3 0651 1.0 / TU 1144 6.3 / 1900 1.1 / 2358 6.5	**18** 0642 0.4 / W 1125 6.9 / 1857 0.6 / 2344 7.1
4 0713 1.0 / W 1211 6.3 / 1920 1.1	**19** 0726 0.4 / TH 1205 6.9 / 1938 0.6
5 0022 6.4 / TH 0734 1.1 / 1234 6.3 / 1943 1.1	**20** 0026 7.0 / F 0805 0.5 / 1249 6.8 / 2017 0.7
6 0041 6.3 / F 0759 1.1 / 1251 6.2 / 2010 1.2	**21** 0110 6.8 / SA 0843 0.8 / 1334 6.5 / 2057 1.0
7 0100 6.3 / SA 0827 1.2 / 1313 6.2 / 2039 1.4	**22** 0157 6.5 / SU 0922 1.2 / 1425 6.1 / 2140 1.4
8 0127 6.2 / SU 0857 1.5 / 1345 6.1 / 2112 1.6	**23** 0251 6.0 / M 1007 1.7 / 1521 5.6 / 2232 1.8
9 0203 5.9 / M 0933 1.7 / 1426 5.8 / 2152 1.9	**24** 0354 5.5 / TU 1101 2.1 / 1626 5.4 / 2343 2.2
10 0250 5.6 / TU 1018 2.1 / 1522 5.4 / 2246 2.2	**25** 1226 2.1 / W 1741 5.2
11 0407 5.1 / W 1122 2.4 / 1729 5.1	**26** 0106 2.2 / TH 0653 5.1 / 1348 2.3 / 1914 5.3
12 0014 2.4 / TH 0625 5.1 / 1857 5.3	**27** 0227 2.0 / F 0814 5.3 / 1500 2.0 / 2023 5.6
13 0158 2.1 / F 0736 5.5 / 1437 2.0 / 2001 5.7	**28** 0333 1.7 / SA 0902 5.6 / 1558 1.7 / 2110 5.9
14 0305 1.6 / SA 0833 5.9 / 1537 1.5 / 2053 6.1	**29** 0427 1.3 / SU 0940 5.9 / 1644 1.5 / 2149 6.1
15 0404 1.2 / SU 0921 6.3 / 1631 1.1 / 2138 6.6	**30** 0506 1.3 / M 1012 6.0 / 1723 1.3 / 2224 6.3

A typical list of monthly tide times. These tide tables are available for all major ports around the coastline.

local to the area you are fishing. Basic tides from a "tide table" are quite simple to understand, but don't be deceived. The tide times in a harbour will not be the same a few miles out to sea over a fishing mark or further along the open coast. Quite often, a distance of 10 miles (16km) offshore or further along the coast, can have up to a three hour difference – high water may well be at 12pm in the harbour, but elsewhere within the locality it could be at 2–3pm. This can make a great difference to the sea conditions and the fishing.

Inside the cover of most local tide times is a list of time adjustments, which can be added or subtracted from the main calculation, for areas between major ports. These adjustments are absolutely essential if you want to find out the correct times for high or low tide in a particular area. On the same day, high and low tides will be at different times at different ports around the coast. Each area has a standard port whereby tide times for each day of the year are predicted. Pick the closest standard port to where you will be fishing and then add or subtract the tidal adjustment, which will usually be given in hours and minutes.

Spring tides and neap tides

There are two types or phases, of tide – springs and neaps.

Spring tides are when the tides will be at their highest and lowest extremes. These are tides where, at low water, estuaries and mud flats dry out and, at high water, the tide often reaches the tops of high harbour walls. Tidal runs will be at their fastest over spring tides, too.

Neap tides are the opposite. The height of high water is lower than spring tides and low waters do not reach the extreme lows. The tidal height difference between low and high water is called the "tidal range" for the day and it is usually measured in metres. Spring tides have a greater range between low and high water than do neap tides. If you ever hear another sea angler say: "today's tide is a 4.2m

At high tide, these boats float happily on a tidal estuary, but they will rest on the mud when the tide recedes six hours later.

or 6.4m", they are talking about the tidal range (the height difference between high and low water) for the day.

Our earth revolves around the sun and the moon revolves around the earth. Spring tides occur when the earth, the moon and the sun are in line and there is maximum gravitation pull. Neaps are the opposite, when the earth, moon and sun are at right angles to one other and the gravitational pull is weakest. The strength in the gravitational pull is directly related to the size of our tides. This lunar cycle, from planet alignment through to planets being at right angles, takes approximately seven days, meaning there are two times every month when the planets are aligned and two times where they are aligned at right angles to one another. This equates to two spring tides and two smaller neap tides per month.

The phases of the lunar cycle can be seen in the night sky by the phase of the moon. Spring tides occur when we have a new or full moon. Neap tides occur when we have a quarter moon or when the moon is in its last quarter. If you've heard another sea angler mention that the fishing is better when there's a full moon, basically they're referring to spring tides. Spring tides often provoke fish to move more and feed harder, although neap tides can make areas with strong tidal flows tamer and easier for the angler and his or her tackle to cope with.

Roughly working out what the tide is doing

Tides have a lot of influence on local fishing. Ask questions about your area, because good fishing tides are generally down to local knowledge – they are very specific to each fishing mark. Understanding basic tides and knowing their times and heights will also allow you to estimate the depth of water, at a given position, for a specific time of the day. Always double check your tides. It would be embarrassing, not to mention dangerous, to run aground in your boat or get cut off while shore fishing from the rocks.

The easiest way to quickly workout what stage of the tide it is and to guess the approximate height at a given time, is to use the "Rule of Twelfths". It takes six hours for the tide to rise and six hours for the tide to fall. These six hours can be divided up into 12 different stages or twelfths. This rule assumes that the tide will rise or fall at a rate of so many twelfths per hour.

1st **hour** 1/12th of the tide rises or falls – tidal flow is at its weakest
2nd **hour** 2/12ths of the tide rises or falls – tidal flow is moderate
3rd **hour** 3/12ths of the tide rises or falls – tidal flow is at its strongest
4th **hour** 3/12ths of the tide rises or falls – tidal flow is at its strongest
5th **hour** 2/12ths of the tide rises or falls – tidal flow is moderate
6th **hour** 1/12th of the tide rises or falls – tidal flow is at its weakest

In summary, spring tides happen twice a month. These are the highest and lowest tides and the tide run will be faster. Neap tides also happen twice a month. Neap tides don't fall so low at low water and don't rise as high at high water. During periods of neap tides, tidal run will be at its weakest, too. Anglers often refer to the incoming tide as the "flood tide" and the outgoing tide as the "ebb tide".

SEA ANGLING CLOTHING AND PERSONAL SAFETY

With such a vast array of weather and sea conditions, it goes without saying that the sea angler needs clothing that is up to the job. On wet and windy days, you'll need clothes that will keep you warm and dry. On sunny days, you'll need clothing that will not only be cool and comfortable but will also offer protection from the harmful solar radiation.

Wet and cold weather angling suits

A wide choice of angling suits are available, including jacket and trousers, bib and brace, smocks and flotation suits. Flotation suits have the added safety factor that they contain buoyancy that will keep you afloat if you are washed in or fall overboard. Many suits have thermal layering for cold weather and others are made from breathable materials for moderate weather.

Pick an angling suit that is visible and comfortable. Mobility is vital. When sea angling from a boat or the shore, a lot of time can be spent kneeling, baiting up or rig making. A suit with reinforced knees and bums is also worth considering, because this is where most suits tend to wear first. Separate thermal suits, gloves, footwear, balaclavas and hats also come in handy. It is always better to wear lots of thin layers that can be removed if needed.

Warm weather clothing

When the weather is hot and sunny, protection from the sun is necessary. Whether you're on a boat, the beach or rocks, the surface of the sea magnifies and intensifies sunlight, which makes sunburn and heatstroke a real threat. Zip off safari-style cargo

Clothing for sea angling comes in many forms. This angler is wearing a suit specifically designed for cold conditions.

trousers are great, as they offer ample storage, yet they can be zipped off at the knees into shorts if you get too hot. Long-sleeved safari-style shirts are also great, being both cool and comfortable and protective from the sun's harmful rays.

Hats and sunglasses

Peaked caps and Polaroid sunglasses not only protect the eyes from glare, but they will also protect the eyes from flying objects such as hooks, lead weights and lures that have been cast incorrectly. Polaroid sunglasses are great, because they reduce reflective surface glare on the water and actually allow you to see up to 20ft (6m) under the water. This is extremely helpful when looking for certain species of fish. Woolly hats will offer warmth in cold conditions, as well as protection in sunny weather.

Caps and sunglasses protect the eyes and head from sunlight and flying objects. Believe it or not, Polaroid sunglasses actually help the sea angler look for fish under the water.

Comfortable footwear is essential for sea angling. Boats and rocks can be slippery places, so you need to make sure the soles are the nonslip variety.

Footwear

Comfortable footwear is essential for sea fishing. This could be walking boots, Wellingtons or an old pair of trainers, depending on where you're fishing and what the weather is like. Whatever your choice, the requirements of good angling footwear are the same. Good fishing footwear needs to be non-slip and offer maneuverability and support. Waders are not essential for sea angling, but they are popular with shore anglers who wish to get out that little bit further from surf beaches and estuaries. A good safety tip to remember is that Wellingtons and waders can be potential hazards if you fall in, because they will fill with sea water, which will make swimming impossible. Always think safety first when choosing your footwear. If you understand weather and the terrain where you will be fishing, you'll know what to wear to keep comfortable and safe.

Life jackets

Life jackets are the most important item of safety equipment for the boat angler. They can also be used when taking children pier or rock fishing. On charter boats and bigger boats with high gunwales (sides!), life jackets do not need to be worn. On small boats, boats with low gunwales and in rough conditions

It is not a legal requirement to wear a life jacket aboard a boat, but it makes sense to wear one, especially if the conditions deteriorate or in boats with low sides. Life jackets should always been worn when taking young anglers shore fishing.

at sea, life jackets should be worn at all times. It is important you wear the right sized life jacket for your body mass, otherwise it won't keep you afloat should you fall in. Make sure your life jacket is fitted properly otherwise it could do more harm than good.

SAFETY

While on the subject of protective clothing for sea angling, it would seem sensible to add a few words on safety. The sea is a place of freedom for all to enjoy, where anything goes. However, at the same time sea angling is a dangerous pastime. All sea anglers should put safety first, fishing second.

Know your weather, know your tides and dress appropriately for the day's conditions. Always ensure you inform somebody of your whereabouts before you go on a fishing expedition. If you plan to fish from a boat, never go to sea without a working VHF marine radio and a qualified radio operator. When shore fishing, always use the buddy system and fish with another angler or where there are other anglers. Do not venture out onto rocks or wade into surf alone.

Some small safety items every sea angler should carry in their pockets or tackle box include a small first aid kit (available from most chemists), a signaling whistle and a torch (which can also be used for signaling). A thermal protective aid (TPA) or a foil blanket (which packs down into a small bag). A TPA can help to reflect body heat to help with shock, for example, following a fall or with hypothermia from submersion. A mobile phone can come in handy to contact the emergency services in the event of an accident. However, remember that phones do not always work from the coast or further offshore, so you may have to travel to get a signal.

Sea fishing is a dangerous sport. Never go to sea onboard a boat that is not fitted with a marine radio. If you're shore fishing, carry simple items like a first aid kit and a mobile phone. These items will be invaluable in the event of an emergency.

THE ULTIMATE GUIDE TO FISHING

SHORE FISHING OR BOAT FISHING?

Large open areas of coastline make great competition venues that can accommodate many anglers fishing against each other.

There are many different types of sea angling, each with its own charms and challenges to suit different personalities. Many sea anglers enjoy the variety of sea fishing and many participate in both shore and boat angling.

Sea angling can also be divided into competitive fishing or fishing for pleasure. Some anglers choose to fish so they can put their feet up, relax and enjoy their surroundings. If they catch, it's a bonus. Others enjoy the challenge of pitting their wits against fellow anglers, as well as the fish.

Competitive sea angling

Sea angling can be assessed in many ways. In some competitions, points are awarded per species and amount of fish. Best specimen competitions are usually judged on the weight of the fish, as a percentage, against the local specimen size for that species. Specimen sea fishing, where the angler seeks bigger and better fish, has become popular in the last decade. Both pleasure and competitive angling can be performed from beaches, piers and rocks and from boats — both onshore and offshore.

Pier fishing

Breakwaters, jetties and piers offer easy access and simple fishing. They are often the first choice for novice anglers or for those wanting an easy afternoons fishing. Find a pier anywhere in Britain or Ireland and there's sure to be fish around somewhere and an angler waiting to catch them. Piers offer great fishing. Whether they are solid walled or erected on piles, they form an obstruction in the tide and this itself attracts the fish. Piers offer a free home for many species of sea fish and also a place in which to feed. Bait fish often seek shelter around piers and the structure attracts plant growth and shellfish, which is the start of the food chain. Breakwaters, jetties and piers attract the full range of fish – surface, midwater and bottom-feeding species.

Piers offer social angling where many anglers will be fishing in close proximity to one another. For this reason, they are great places for newcomers to come and learn from more experienced anglers. Piers also make great competition venues. Having many competing anglers in one place, where many species can be caught, not only means a successful competition but also one that can be adjudicated simply and safely. Some of the best pier fishing can be found over the summer months for species such as black bream, garfish, mackerel, and mullet.

Piers offer safe, simple and social fishing – great for novice and disabled anglers.

THE ULTIMATE GUIDE TO FISHING

Beach fishing

Beach fishing allows an angler to get away from it all. Some large beaches can be found on the seafronts of large towns and small secret coves are tucked away further along many coastlines. Beaches offer challenging fishing for the sea angler. With the exception of lure fishing, beach fishing is usually for bottom-feeding species. Different species will be present on different beaches and each beach will have its own particular characteristics, which may involve long or short-distance casting. Some beaches offer excellent lure fishing for bass, especially in the southern counties of Britain during summer and the autumn. Many beaches offer great fishing over the winter.

Many sea anglers enjoy beach fishing because it requires a higher level of rig making and bait-presentation skills. Beaches also make good, safe competition venues. Beach fishing can be great for species such as bass, codling, dogfish and whiting, as well as the many varieties of flatfish and rays.

Beaches make excellent venues for anglers who want to explore fishing for bottom feeders such as cod, flatfish and rays.

Rock fishing

Rock fishing is for the shore angler, who not only wants to pit his wits against fish, but also the rugged environment. Good rock fishing can be found along most coastlines. Rocks can offer varied fishing for many different species, because the terrain under the water line can be just as varied. Some rock fishing marks offer deepwater, while others offer shallow water. Some rock fishing marks offer casting over reefs, while others offer casting over soft sand. Rock marks can attract surface, midwater and bottom-feeding fish species.

Many sea anglers enjoy rock fishing for peace and quiet and for the added challenges this tough environment can add to the difficulties in playing and landing a fish. Rock fishing does not make safe competition fishing for obvious reasons. Rock fishing can be great for hard-fighting species, such as ballan wrasse, bull huss and conger.

BOATS USED FOR FISHING

Boat fishing is an increasingly popular form of sea fishing for many reasons. It gives the angler increased

Rock fishing offers the sea angler the ultimate challenge — tough terrain and big fish.

Boats used for fishing differ greatly from pleasure craft. Fishing boats usually have lots more deck space, giving the angler more room to move around. Large fishing boats have wheelhouses; smaller boats have cuddies.

scope to range further afield in search of his or her quarry. It provides freedom — away from the hustle and bustle of everyday life. And it provides further challenges for the angler than just fishing. The sea angler must understand boats, seamanship and navigation. He also must become competent at operating the sophisticated electronics that are now common on modern boats. It is possible to catch fish from any boat but, with modern technology, many water craft have been specifically designed for fishing.

Boats that are designed for fishing will have more deck space. Time and money is invested into developing boat hulls that offer sea keeping, speed and stability. Inside the wheelhouse of any boat, it is common to see a Global Positioning System (GPS) and a radar system. An angling boat will also have an echo sounder to locate the fish.

Rod holders are important on the deck of an angling boat and there are different versions to store rods and ones to support a rod while fishing. A cutting board is vital to prepare bait and fillet any catch kept for the table, as is a cool box to keep the bait and the catch fresh. On the subject of bait, a purpose bait tank with an aeration system is necessary to use live-bait. Many angling boat manufacturers will offer all these options installed as standard or as custom details.

Inshore boat fishing

Although some charter boats specialise in inshore fishing, it is the small private boat angler who takes better advantage of our seas out to a few miles (inshore). Good inshore boat fishing can be found from all coasts.

Anglers on this small boat are taking advantage of the wonderful fishing that can be found just out of reach from the shore angler. Great inshore boat fishing can be found around most coastlines.

For the inshore boat angler, wreck reef and sand bank fishing is available within a short distance of the coast. You can fish for a wide variety of species if the weather is good. If the weather is bad, many small boat skippers will turn to inshore harbours and estuaries which, in turn, offer different challenges and different fish species. Small boat anglers regularly target surface, midwater and bottom-feeding species.

Many sea anglers enjoy the freedom of owning their own boat to explore the waters outside of casting distance from the shore. There are lots of private angling boat clubs, facilities and competitions, where assistance can be found. Small boat anglers regularly target species such as bass, cod, flatfish, rays, smooth hounds and tope.

Offshore boat fishing

Many sea anglers do not own a boat, let alone one big enough to venture a long way offshore. If you want to fish the deep seas beyond the horizon, the likelihood is that you'll have to book a charter boat with a professional skipper. Charter boats usually have to be certified and each skipper will need to hold an appropriate license. When booking a charter fishing trip, remember to ask questions. Some skippers specialise in certain types of fishing, while others specialise in specific species.

Every day of the year, charter boats depart from ports all around the coast in search of the best fishing for their angling customers. The list of species that charter boats target is extensive and many boats offer a fishing style instead, often named for the type of seabed marks that you'll be fishing over. These are self explanatory – mixed ground, reef, sandbank, wreck and shark fishing.

Offshore charter fishing boats with professional skippers can be found operating from most ports around the coastline.

SEA FISHING TACKLE

The different forms of sea fishing are unique. It's important that the angler has the correct rod for the type of fishing he or she is intending.

Sea fishing tackle is unlike coarse fishing tackle which, in turn, is unlike fly fishing tackle. Relatively little can be transferred between the different disciplines, with the exception of tackle needed for mullet fishing. If you wish to take up sea fishing, you're going to need a rod, a reel, an appropriate strength line, some end tackle (this is the name for the tackle components you attach to the end of your line to attract and catch fish) and something to carry everything in.

As your sea fishing improves, you'll probably progress through different types of rod and reel until you find a set-up you feel comfortable with. If you find yourself enjoying more than one type of sea fishing, for example, inshore boat fishing and shore fishing, you'll almost certainly need more than one fishing rod and reel, different lines and lots of different end-tackle components.

Sea fishing rods

All sea fishing rods share similar characteristics and the same basic components. They are a pole, usually made of fibreglass, high modulus carbon fibre or a composite, with the latter being modern and lighter.

Each rod requires guides (rings) to carry the line, a reel seat or similar device to hold the reel in position and some form of grip to hold when casting and playing fish. Rod grips can be made from materials such as cork, Duplon and Eva foam.

Each type of rod will have a different length, quantity of line guides and action (the bending curve), all of which depend on the type of fishing and species it is to be used for. The "action" of a rod refers to the responsiveness of the rods bending curve and the speed with which the rod returns to its straight position. An action may be slow, medium or fast or a combination of two, for example, "a medium-fast action". Fast-action rods flex most in the tip section. Slow or "through-action", rods flex all the way through to the butt of the rod.

With two types of fishing reel commonly used – multiplier and fixed spool – most sea fishing rods are usually made to use with one type of reel only. Rods made for multiplier reels require more line guides than rods made for fixed spool reels. Rods made for fixed spool reels require larger line guides than their counterparts.

Casting and striking

A fishing rod is designed to do several things. Firstly, it allows an angler to play a fish. The length and action (stiffness) of the rod give an angler the control he or she needs when fighting any fish that is hooked, with the rod cushioning any lunges the fish may make. However, the main uses of a fishing rod are to assist casting and striking.

Shore and boat fishing rods differ. Longer-distance casting is rarely needed from a boat and therefore boat fishing rods are generally much shorter in length.

An angler performs an off-the-ground cast. It is important for the shore angler to master casting.

Longer rods are generally developed for long-distance casting. Shorter rods are for short chucks or dropping baits over the side of a boat or pier. Casting for a sea angler is very important. A small number of sea anglers practise casting as a professional sport in its own right.

The simplest cast to perform, when starting shore angling, is the overhead thump. This is also used by boat anglers who "uptide" fish. To gain extra distance, many beach anglers use an "off-the-ground" cast.

For professional casters and rock anglers, nothing compares to a pendulum cast, which is the most difficult to master but can propel fishing baits to more than 597ft (182m). For novice anglers, casting will be far easier to master using a fixed spool type real than a multiplier reel, as the latter can be prone to over-runs. Over-runs or "bird-nests", as they are otherwise known, occur when the line comes off the reel too fast and creates a tangle around the spool.

Striking is used after a bite is seen or felt. To strike, the angler lifts or sweeps the rod quickly to take up any slack line and pull the hook so that its point sets into the jaw of the fish. Striking is used a lot in sea angling, but it is not always necessary. Whether you need to strike, or not, often depends on the fish species you're targeting, the weather conditions, the depth of catch and the type of hooks you are using. Some modern hooks, such as circle hooks, have the ability to set themselves as a fish takes the bait and swims away.

Novice anglers should first start by learning the overhead thump. First, face the target area with the rod, reel and bait ready to cast.

Second, swiftly and smoothly sweep the rod forward. This will make the rod compress with the motion and weight of the bait.

Finally, as the rod comes "overhead" and in front of you, around the 2pm position, release the line to complete the cast.

Pier fishing rods are specially designed for short casts in close proximity to other anglers.

Beach fishing rods are the longest of all sea fishing rods. The length is needed to help the angler cast to greater distances.

SHORE FISHING RODS

Rods that are to be used from the coastline can simply be dived into three categories – pier, beach and rough ground.

Pier rods

Pier fishing rods are usually 9-10ft (2.7–3m) long. The action of the rod allows the angler to cast small to medium-sized baits, short to medium distances and are not cumbersome when used near other anglers. Pier rods are often built for use with fixed spool reels and they are suitable for both float-and bottom-fishing.

Beach rods

Beach fishing rods are usually 12–14ft (3.6–4.3m) long, with some long-distance casting rods measuring up to 18ft (5.5m). The action is often rated on how much lead is optimally required to load the rod (bend it under pressure when casting) and gain maximum casting distance. This could be anything from 4–8ozs (113–226g). Beach rods are made for both multiplier and fixed spool reels. They have a sensitive tip for bite detection, so they are almost exclusively used for bottom-fishing.

Rough-ground rods

Rough-ground rods are similar to beach fishing rods in that they are usually 12–14ft (3.6–4.3m) long. However, the action and construction of a rough-ground rod is much heavier. Rough-ground rods will often be used to cast as much as 10–12ozs (283–340g) and the force that may have to be put on a rough-ground rod to stop fish running back into rocks means that these rods need great strength to take the strain. Most rough-ground rods are made for use in conjunction with multiplier reels and they are only suitable for bottom-fishing.

Rods made for rough-ground rock fishing have to be tough to cope with the terrain over which they are used.

BOAT FISHING RODS

Boat fishing rods can be divided into two categories and each is simple to remember. Down-tide (standard boat) rods are shorter and are made to lower baits over the side of a boat, down tide. Up-tide rods are longer and, as the name implies, are designed to cast baits from a boat up-tide.

Down-tide boat fishing rods

Down-tide rods usually range from 6–8ft (1.8–2.4m), but some manufacturers make rods as long as 10ft (3m). Down-tide rods, shorter than 6ft (1.8m), are often called stand-up rods. The action of a down-tide rod is measured by the test curve. This is a description that is used to calibrate how much weight is required to pull a rod blank tip until it is 90 degrees to the butt. The blank would be fixed horizontally and weights fixed to the tip until the 90 degrees is reached. Whatever the total weight, in pounds and ounces, that is required to achieve this is called the rods "test curve". Typical test curves for boats rods include 6lb (2.7kg), 12lb (5.5kg), 15lb (6.8kg), 20lb (9kg), 30lb (13.6kg) and 50lb (22.7kg) class or a combination of two, for example, 12–20lb (5.5–9kg) class.

This way of rating the action of a down-tide rod in pounds is not indicative of the size of fish that the rod was intended for. It is possible to catch fish as large as 100lb (45.5kg) on a 20lb (9kg) class boat rod. The greater the depth of water, the more weight needed to carry the bait to the seabed. These will be the determining factors when choosing the rod action needed to fish comfortably. Down-tide rods are always made to use with multiplier reels.

Up-tide boat fishing rods

Up-tide rods are usually around 9½ft (2.9m) long. Up-tide boat rods are longer than down-tide boat rods because the extra length is needed to cast baits away from a boat up tide. Up-tide rods are similar

A boat fishing rods' strength and action is measured by the test curve. Lighter test curve rods are used for small fish and heavy test curves for big fish!

to beach fishing rods because they are also rated on how much lead is optimally required to load the rod (bend it under pressure when casting) to gain casting distance. This could be anything from 4–10oz (0.1–2.8kg). Up-tide rods are usually available in fixed spool or multiplier reel versions and they make extremely versatile boat fishing rods because they can also be used to fish down tide.

Miscellaneous sea fishing rods

For certain types of sea fishing and for certain types of fish, you'll require a specialist rod. Specialist rods range from spinning and plug-lure fishing rods, through bass rods, flatfish rods and mullet-fishing rods, to travel rods.

Up-tide rods are longer than down-tide rods because they are designed to cast baits "up tide" from the boat.

Lure fishing rods

Lure fishing rods (often called spinning and plugging rods) range from 7-12ft (2.2–3.7m) long and are usually rated by the weight of lure they can cast. This can be anything from 0.3oz (10g) to lures in excess of 3.5oz (100g). Lure fishing rods are generally made for fixed spool reel use only, with the exception of bait-caster rods, which are made for use with a small multiplier reel instead.

Lure fishing rods are mainly used to cast spinners and plugs. As a result, they are also known as spinning and plugging rods.

Bass and flatfish fishing rods

Bass and flatfish rods are very similar. Both are made in lengths from 11–12ft (3.4–3.7m). Bass and flatfish rods are designed to be lighter to fish over a shallow, featureless seabed, at short casting distances where they will give better sport and greater control over the fight. Bass and flatfish rods are rated on the weight they can cast, which is usually between 2–5oz (56–142g) and both are made in fixed spool and multiplier reel versions.

Bass and flatfish fishing rods have to be light, because this type of fishing requires the angler to hold the rod, feeling for a bite, for long periods.

Mullet fishing rods

Mullet fishing rods and other float fishing rods are specialist rods and are scarce in the stores, so often sea anglers will use a coarse fishing (barbel or feeder) rod instead. A good rod for light tackle fishing will measure 11–12ft (3.4–3.7m) long and rated with a test-curve between 1.5 and 1.75lb (0.7 and 0.8kg). These specialist coarse fishing rods are made for use with fixed spool reels only.

Travel rods

Very few fishing rods are single piece – most are made up of two or three sections that are connected together using spigot or put-over joints. Travel rods are very similar but to maximise the rod in its collapsed state (travel size), travel rods are created stronger and are made of four to six sections

Specialist mullet rods are difficult to find. For mullet fishing, the sea angler often has to adopt a coarse-fishing feeder rod instead.

of shorter lengths. Travel rods always come in a protective travel tube and are great when size and weight are an issue. This could be to fit in the back of the car, to take on public transport or backpacking

when travelling overseas where baggage allowances on aircraft can be restrictive.

SEA FISHING REELS

As mentioned under sea fishing rods, sea fishing reels come in two varieties. Each one has a specific use, as well as a rod to pair with. When purchasing a sea fishing reel, it is important to get the correct type and size of reel, or both the rod and reel will be unbalanced and uncomfortable to hold. It is also worth bearing in mind what line you'll need for the fishing you intend to do. All fishing reels, both fixed spool and multiplier versions, have different spool sizes that hold different capacities of line.

A spinning reel – note that the spool is in line with the rod.

All fishing reels have a way to release line. This is the bail arm on fixed spool reels. On multiplier reels you need to disengage a lever to release the line. A reel also needs a drag to fight and tire the fish which will stop the fish from breaking the line. This is a clutch system that allows a fish to take line, under pressure, while the angler is fighting it using

Multiplier reels with their spools at right angles to the direction of the rod.

the rod. Finally, the most important thing of all, every sea fishing reel needs to have a handle to reel in your catch.

The main difference between a multiplier reel and a fixed spool reel is the way the reel works to expel and retrieve fishing lines. On a multiplier reel, the reel spool is at a right angle to the rod and rotates when line is taken or retrieved. On a fixed spool reel, the reel spool is in line with the rod, but instead of the reel spool revolving, the spool is fixed. The weight of the end tackle and bait or a lure, peels the monofilament line sideways off the spool when cast and, when retrieved, the bail arm and its guide rotate around the spool and lay the line instead of the spool turning itself.

Both multiplier and fixed spool reels are available with different line retrieve ratios. Slow reels take up line at a rate of perhaps three to four revolutions of the spool to one rotation of the reel handle. Fast retrieve reels can make five, six or even more revolutions of the spool to one rotation of the fishing reel handle. Multiplier reels are great for deep-sea boat fishing, long-range beach casting and rock fishing. Fixed spool reels are suited to close-range and shallow-water fishing, lure fishing and other light-tackle fishing from both boat and shore.

LINES AND LEADERS

Many anglers spend a lot of time choosing the right rod and reel, but one of the most important parts of a sea angler's tackle is the line. The line is the main link between the angler and his or her catch

and there are a few considerations to make before choosing a fishing line.

Fishing lines come in different thicknesses and strengths. A strong line will hold any fish and offer abrasion resistance. However, some fish can see thick lines and thick lines also get swept by strong tide. As a result, you'll often have to adopt lighter line tactics. There are also two types of line constructed using different materials — monofilament and braid.

Mono (monofilament)

Monofilament is strong and supple. It knots well and comes in different colours, breaking strains and diametres. A breaking strain is the rating at which the line should break when under pressure. This is directly related to the diametre of the line. Stronger lines are thicker — weaker lines are thinner. Popular monofilament breaking strains for sea angling include 8lb (3.6kg), 10lb (4.5kg), 12lb (5.5kg), 15lb (6.8kg), 18lb (8.2kg), 20lb (9kg), 25lb (11.4kg), 30lb (13.6kg) and 50lb (22.7kg). Lighter lines are used for lure and light-tackle fishing. Medium-rated lines, from 15–25lb (6.8–11.4kg), are used for general shore and boat angling. Heavier lines are used for rough-ground and big-fish fishing. Monofilament is reliable and cheap. However, it is thick and catches in the tide, so there is reduced contact between the angler and fish.

The line is the main connection between angler and the fish. Always make sure you use high-quality line on your reels and rigs.

THE ULTIMATE GUIDE TO FISHING

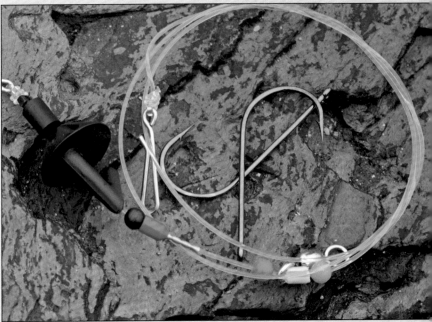

Braid has revolutionised sea angling. It is thinner than monofilament, stronger and has no stretch, which means it gives greater bite detection.

A pulley rig constructed using high-quality monofilament, snood and leader lines.

Braid

Braided lines have revolutionised sea angling over the past decade. Braid differs from monofilament in that it is made by spinning polyethylene fibres to create a very low diametre fishing line that is strong, thin and has no stretch (in contrast to monofilament line). Braid comes in fewer breaking strains than monofilament, including 8lb (3.6kg), 10lb (4.5kg), 15lb (6.8kg), 20lb (9kg), 30lb (13.6kg) and 50lb (22.7kg). Again, the lower breaking strains of braid are used for specialist fishing, the medium-rated lines for general sea fishing and the heavier-braided lines for bigger species of fish.

Braided lines, with their low stretch, are great for bite detection. The low diametre/high breaking strain ratio in which braid is available means that it has superior tide-cutting ability without compromising the strength. For example, a 20lb (9kg) braid has the same diametre of 6lb (2.7kg) breaking strain monofilament. However, braid is more expensive than monofilament and can damage more easily.

LEADERS AND TRACES

Shore anglers often tie on a shock leader, which is a length of heavier monofilament added to the end of their reel lines. This is to take the shock from the power applied to a strong cast. Anglers who use braided lines often tie a monofilament leader to the end of their braid. This helps a little with shock absorption and also with seabed abrasion on this expensive line.

Traces, hook-links and snoods are names for the length of line to which the hook is attached. In general, different breaking strains of monofilament line, balanced against how hard a fish fights and the likelihood of it biting through the line, are used for most sea fishing. For some big species, such as sharks, multistrand wire line is used to combat their sharp teeth. Monofilament traces can be knotted. Wire traces have to be joined using crimps.

In recent years a new type of leader and trace line has become available and can be used in place of monofilament (not wire). Fluorocarbon is a high-tech line that has the same refractive index as water and is invisible to fish. Anything that slows the speed at which light travels, such as line, will become visible underwater. Unlike monofilament lines, fluorocarbon is uniquely invisible because light travels through it at almost the same speed as it naturally travels through water. Fluorocarbon is very expensive, however, but it is necessary for any species that is a wary feeder.

END TACKLE

When a sea angler refers to end tackle, he or she is talking about the items that are tied to the "end" of the line, usually composed into a rig, which will be baited to attract the fish.

Hooks

Hooks come in many patterns and sizes. Hook variations include the length of the hook shank and the width of the hook (the gape). Some hooks are chemically sharpened, for example, those made from carbon steel. Avoid hooks made from stainless steel because if they are left in a fish or lost, they do not rust away in the same way as hooks made from other materials. Popular hook patterns include O'Shaughnessy, Viking, Wide Gape, Treble and Circle hooks. Each one has a different shank, gape, eye and barb. Circle hooks are a relatively new hook pattern. The shape guarantees that a fish is hooked in the jaw and not deeper in the throat or even gut, which means they are great for catch and release fishing. Popular sea fishing hooks range from size 1 and 1/0 through to 10/0. The smaller size 1 and 1/0 hooks are used for small species, with 2/0 to 6/0 widely used for general sea fishing. The larger 7/0 to 10/0 hooks are only used for big sea fish. The pattern and size of hook that you'll need will be determined by the species you are fishing for. Small hooks suit smaller species, while big hooks are stronger so that they can cope with the weight of big fish. Coarse fishing hooks are needed for mullet fishing.

Keep your hooks in a plastic box with dividing compartments to separate the hooks by type and size.

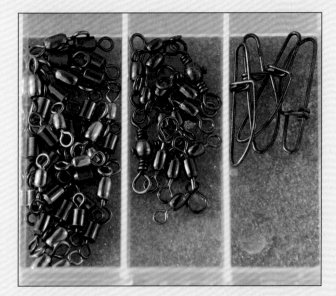

Swivels are essential for making most sea fishing rigs. A swivel adds rotational movement to a rig, which can help decrease line tangles and create better bait presentation.

Swivels

A swivel is a device of two halves, each of which can rotate independently. Swivels are used in the line to allow rotational movement to the rig or end tackle to decrease rig tangles and for a more natural bait presentation. Similar to hooks, swivels come in a range of sizes and it is best to use the smallest possible, keeping your end tackle and rig as invisible as it can be.

Snap link swivels

Snap link swivels have a clip on one end that can be opened and then shut to attach other end tackle components, such as lures and weights, to the line.

Beads

Plastic and rubber beads are often threaded onto the line to protect knots from sliding end-tackle components, such as booms. Beads of different colours and sizes can also be used to attract certain species of sea fish.

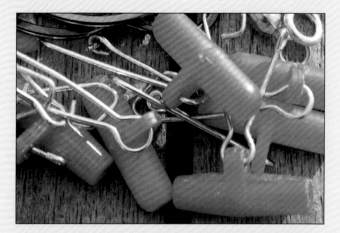

Booms are essential for boat angling. Using a boom helps to stop trace lines tangling around the mainline when a bait is dropped from a boat to the seabed.

Booms

A boom is a plastic or metal device to which a trace and hook is added. Using a boom when fishing in deep water or with long traces, can greatly reduce tangles in the line. Many booms come with a snap link swivel or clip, to which any necessary weight can be directly attached.

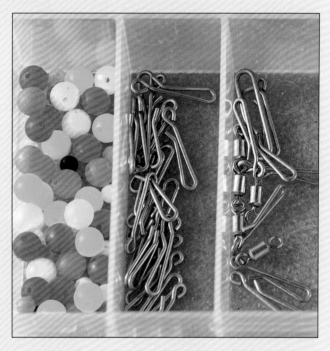

Beads protect knots from sliding tackle components and they also attract some sea fish species.

Crimps

Small metal crimps are often used by shore anglers to hold the line in place instead of knots. Wire lines, which cannot be knotted, have to be crimped in place. They are used for predatory fish such as sharks.

Floats

A float is a buoyant rig component that is used to suspend baits up in the water column and off the seabed. Floats are exciting to fish with because the angler has to watch the float for bite indication.

Feathers

Feathers are "flylike" lures, which are tied into a readymade rig, where often three to six feathers are used together to attract and catch shoaling fish such as mackerel. Feathers can also be used to collect bait like sandeels. They can also be baited and used to catch small seabed feeding species.

A boat angler uses feathers to catch mackerel — more than one at a time.

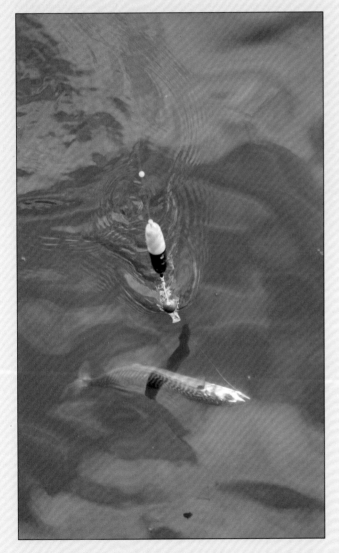

A float is a buoyant rig component used to suspend baits up in the water column. The float is specifically used for surface and midwater feeding species.

Weights, otherwise known as sinkers, are an important item of end tackle. Without weights it would be impossible to fish in deep water.

Lead weights

One of the most important end-tackle components is the weight or sinker, which is used to help the bait descend. Small ball-weights are used to cock (right) fishing floats. Pear-shaped leads from 1–4oz (28–113g) are used with light-tackle fishing rods. Popular sized leads with beach anglers range from 5–8oz (141–226g) and gripper weights have wire prongs which anchor them to the seabed. For boat fishing, 6–12oz (170–340g) leads are commonly used to get the bait to the seabed. However, up to 1–2lb (0.4–0.8kg) of lead can be required in deepwater or fast tides.

LUGGAGE AND ACCESSORIES

You need something to carry your tackle in to keep it organised, tidy and ready to go. Most fishing tackle manufacturers make a wide variety of tackle bags, tackle boxes and other storage systems.

Pleasure anglers usually make do with a tool-box style tackle box. Beach anglers prefer a tackle box that they can also use as a seat. Lure anglers and rock anglers, who are always on the move, prefer a rucksack style bag in which to carry their tackle. For boat angling, a good waterproof box or bag is required to protect the fishing tackle from the corrosive sea spray. Plastic trays with dividers and rig wallets are used by most sea anglers to keep end tackle components and ready-made rigs separate and tangle free. In addition to a tackle box, a good investment is a rod hold-all to protect fishing rods (if you have more than one rod), as well as reel covers to protect the different fishing reels.

For all types of fishing, you're going to need a tackle box to keep everything in. Shore anglers favour seat boxes like this one. Boat anglers often use smaller tackle boxes that take up less room on a boat deck.

Plastic trays and rig wallets are used by both shore and boat anglers to keep end tackle items and ready-made rigs separate and tangle free.

Where boats nearly always have fitted rod rests and shelter under a cuddy or wheelhouse, the shore angler may want to consider using a rod rest to hold his rods upright when fishing and an umbrella or shelter for comfort and protection.

Some other accessories to make life easier for the general sea angler include a pair of snips to cut lines, pliers to make rigs and a disgorger to remove hooks from fish. Containers in which to carry bait are handy, as is a sharp knife to prepare baits. If you intend using live bait, then a purpose bait tank, with battery operated aeration pump, will keep live-bait healthy all day. For most types of sea angling, a landing net will be helpful.

SEA FISHING BAITS

Common shore crabs can be deadly bait for many types of sea fish species.

The key to successful lure fishing is to try to represent the bait that the fish are currently feeding on.

Similar to coarse fishing, there are two types of bait a sea angler can use to attract fish. They are natural baits, which are baits that are found in the local area and artificial baits, which are made to look, act or smell like natural baits.

HOW FISH HUNT

Every species of fish has three main objectives in life — to reproduce and to survive long enough to reproduce without getting eaten. When they are not doing those things, most fish are usually feeding.

Different fish species feed using different methods to sense food and this can often be deduced from shape and biology of the fish.

With the exception of sharks and eel-like fishes, longer, streamlined fish with large tails that spend much of their time up in the water are usually active predators. These fish are often coloured and patterned to camouflage them in their surroundings. Alternatively, they are silver to reflect light, which also makes them camouflaged from the fish they are hunting. All active predators have sensitive lateral lines, which run along each flank of the fish, from

head to tail. The lateral lines are used to detect movement in the water. Predatory fish also have large eyes to spot their prey and a mouth suitable for engulfing whole foods such as small baitfish. Some predatory species, especially those which feed among shoals of baitfish, often have a protruding lower jaw, making catching food easier.

Flatter and rounder fish have developed to spend much of their time gliding and slowly swimming on the seabed. These fish are coloured to blend in with their surroundings, but this is often for protection. Many bottom-feeding fish hunt for food by smell, using their nares (nostrils) and scent receptors, which are located all over the snout and sometimes on the body. The mouths of many bottom-feeding species are either on the fish's undersides or angled downward to make bottom-feeding easier.

You can tell a lot from the shape and distinguishing features of each species. To catch specific fish, it is important to understand each species and where it feeds. You can then select the appropriate bait and present it to them in the method that would be most natural for that area.

NATURAL BAITS

There are many natural types of bait available that the sea angler can collect and/or purchase from a good tackle store.

Marine worms

Rag worm is one of the most common sea fishing baits and can be dug from rough estuarine beaches or bought by weight.

Lugworm is a different type of marine worm, which can be dug from sandy beaches and softer estuarine areas. Lugworm is a very good beach fishing bait and can also be purchased from good tackle stores.

LEFT: *Rag worm is one of the most commonly used baits in sea fishing and is great for many fish species.*

BELOW: *You can dig up lugworm from sandy beaches and softer estuarine areas.*

All crabs must shed their shell once a year to grow. When they do, the soft-shelled crabs are called "peeler" crabs and most fish find them irresistible.

Squid is great bait for big fish. An angler has baited with three squid hoping to catch a big conger eel.

Live sandeels are great bait for summer species such as bass. Frozen sandeels, which can be purchased from all good tackle stores, come a close second best.

Crab

Common shore crabs are great bait for certain species. Common shore crabs have to shed their shells to grow in size and in this soft form they are known as peeler crabs. Many fish find peeler crabs irresistible. Although they can be collected along rocky and weedy coastlines, some tackle stores are able to supply them for sale. Hardback common crabs, which are not ready to or have already shed their shells and grown new ones, also make good baits for certain species at different times of the year.

Squid and cuttlefish

Squid and cuttlefish are difficult for the angler to collect, but they are readily available for purchase. Both can be used whole for big fish or cut into smaller baits for smaller species.

Sandeel and launce

Sandeels are great bait for summer species such as bass. Sandeels can be collected from the coast, but this is very difficult. Some tackle stores in specific areas will supply live sandeels in small quantities. Boat anglers are able to collect their own sandeels easily, using a set of small feathers and jigging them close to the bottom over sandbanks and reefs. The sand eel comes in two varieties. The lesser sandeel is small and has a brown back. Greater sandeels (launce) are bigger and have green backs. Sandeels can be used dead or alive. Live eels will need to be kept in a purpose bait tank with an aerator.

Mackerel

Mackerel is a common bait used by sea anglers because they are easily available and easy to catch. Like cuttlefish and squid, mackerel can also be bought from fishing tackle stores blast frozen in packs. Mackerel can be used whole, live or dead or filleted and cut into chunks or slithers. Mackerel flapper bait is when a whole mackerel is filleted but only as far as the head, the fish sides are left attached with the backbone removed. A mackerel flapper bait releases scent and "flaps" around enticingly in the tide. This bait works very well for big fish such as conger, ling and sharks.

Prawn

Prawns are not widely used but they make great sea angling baits for aggressive species such as bass and sea wrasse. Prawns are used live by hooking them through the tail or dead by threading them on a hook like a worm.

Mackerel is a versatile bait that can be caught or bought; used whole live or dead or cut into chunks or strips.

Shellfish

Many types of shellfish, such as clams, limpets and mussels, can be collected and used as bait. Difficult-to-collect shellfish, such as razorfish, can often be bought in frozen packs from tackle stores. Shellfish baits can be used whole or cut to tip off other baits.

Combination and tip baits

Combination baits are two or more baits used in conjunction with one another. One of the favourable combination baits of the sea angler is lugworm and peeler crab, which is used for big cod.

A tip bait is a small cut of bait used to "tip off" another bait. The most famous of these is rag worm tipped with a squid strip. This is an excellent tactic for flatfish such as plaice.

Baiting elastic

Baiting elastic is a microfibre elastic thread that can be wound around large soft baits to secure them more firmly on the hook.

ARTIFICIAL BAITS (LURES)

Artificial baits are designed to represent natural baits when moved through the water. Artificial baits have been around since fishing began. In recent years, they have become increasingly popular with specialist sea anglers, particularly those who seek bass.

All artificial baits are shaped and coloured to look like the real bait that they are intended to replicate, although some artificial baits can be bright and fluorescent, which can be provocative to some species on some days or in certain areas. With most artificial baits, the angler has to retrieve line and impart an action into the bait to make it act in a lifelike manner.

Combination baits are when two or more baits are used in conjunction with one another.

Scented baits

Baits that attract by scent only, often made from rubber impregnated with scented oil, have been around for many years. As yet, the perfect scented replica has not been found. Scent additives, which can be applied to enhance natural baits, are successful with fish species that hunt using smell as a primary method of detecting food.

Soft baits

Latex and rubber baits, known as "soft baits", have grown in popularity in recent years. The durability of these materials means they can be moulded into realistic bait shapes and coloured accordingly with great detail. Soft baits are designed to swim naturally when retrieved by the angler. Another property of the rubber used in the construction of these baits is that it moves in a lifelike manner when in the water. Soft baits come in all shapes and sizes, ranging from worms to crab and small fish.

Some soft-baits come with fitted hooks and some even have an integral weight inside them to aid casting and sinking.

The durability of latex and other rubbers means that they can be moulded into realistic bait shapes.

Hard baits

Hard baits are the opposite of soft-baits. Traditionally, hard baits were made of wood but modern versions are often made of hard plastics.

Hard baits are shaped and coloured to represent natural baits and come in vivid colours. Hard baits are designed to swim naturally when retrieved by the angler. Some float on the surface, while others dive to predetermined depths. Hard baits usually come fitted with treble hooks.

Traditional hard baits were carved from wood. Today, they are made from modern plastics and are almost as realistic as the fish they are made to represent.

Pirks, jigs, spinners and spoons

Along with wood, plastics and rubber, metal can also be used to make artificial baits. Pirks and jigs are large metal artificial baits often used by boat anglers to fish the seabed. Spinners and spoons are smaller metal baits that can be cast and retrieved from both boats and the shore. The reflective properties of most metal artificial baits mean that, when retrieved through the water, they flash like a fish would naturally. Nearly all pirks, jigs and spinners come with prefitted hooks.

DAY-TO-DAY KNOTS

Any knot is a weak point between the angler and the fish, so tying a good knot is vital. Take time to learn a handful of good knots. It will pay dividends in the long run, with less fish lost due to failure. Many knots are specific to the job they were intended for, such as joining lines or attaching items of end tackle.

In reality, there are very few knots a sea angler needs to know to cover every eventuality and, once you've learned a few knots, you'll find many others are based around them or are tied in a similar fashion. Here are four knots to get you going. Try practising them one evening when you're not working or fishing.

The Tucked Half Blood Knot is a great knot for joining lines to tackle components. It is strong, versatile and is regularly used by sea anglers.

The Uni to Uni Knot is a simple knot for joining two lines together or tying a mainline to a leader.

The Rapala Knot is a non-slip loop knot designed to connect lures. The loop in this knot assists a lure by allowing it more movement, which also helps avoid line tangles.

The Dropper Loop Knot can be used to tie snoods onto which a hook can be tied to make a paternoster rig. Paternoster rigs often contain more than one hook, similar to feathers.

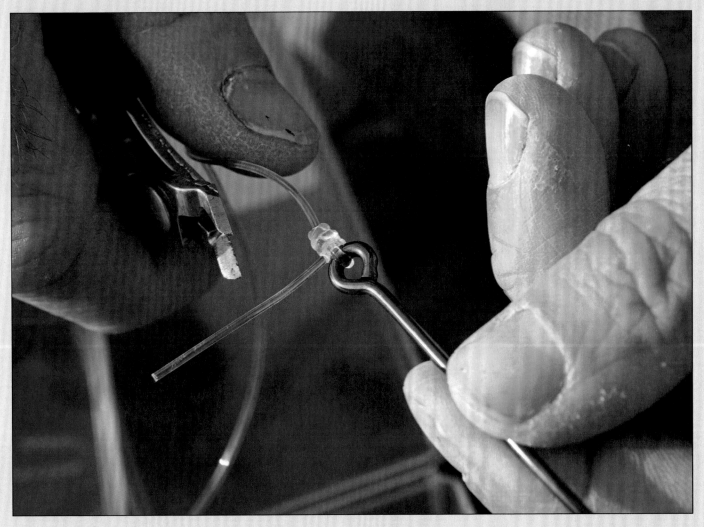

Every sea angler should perfect certain knots. A poorly tied knot could be the big fish that got away.

BASIC SEA FISHING
TECHNIQUES AND
SIMPLE RIGS

Knowing your fish and what rig attracts or provokes them to bite will help you become a successful sea angler.

Different fish species live and survive in different areas, at different depths and over varied underwater terrains. As a result, a sea angler must be able to master certain techniques if he or she wants to catch a variety of different fish.

Rigs also play a big part in sea fishing. When you have located certain species, where they live and feed, you'll then need an effective rig to present your bait as naturally as possible. Many rigs are developed around one simple rig that has been designed to cope with one method of sea angling. Here are the four main methods of sea angling and the simplest, yet most effective, rigs to execute them.

Surface fishing

To fish the surface waters and just beneath the surface is the simplest method for the sea angler to employ and is often called free-lining.

A monofilament leader is tied to the mainline using a small swivel. The hook is attached to the other end of this leader. Free-lining is always used with natural baits, usually live baits. Without hindrance of a lead weight, the free-line rig allows the bait to move with the tide, giving a near-perfect presentation. Small ball leads can be added to the free-line rig to help with strong tides and a bubble float can be added to aid casting distance if needed.

Float fishing

Many summer species prefer to dwell in the warmer, upper layers of the water. The only way to keep a bait floating midwater is to use a float to suspend it there.

A simple float is threaded up the line along with the correct weight to cock the float, then follows a bead, a swivel, a short trace and a hook. A rubber band or stop knot is placed above the float, on the line, which is used to set the depth to which the weight is allowed to sink to. This simple float rig can be cast and used to fish as deep as 20ft (6m).

Float fishing is one of the most exciting but simplest ways to fish the ocean.

Lure fishing

Making a lure move realistically through the water is an art. The lure needs to be fished from a correct rig to achieve this.

When shore fishing, lures are usually tied directly to the mainline or an attached leader. When boat fishing at great depths, a simple rig, called a flying collar rig, is used to take lures to the seabed with the minimum of tangles.

A boom is threaded or tied to the mainline and the required lead weight is attached using a snap link swivel to reach the seabed. After the boom, a length of trace is tied, which can vary between 2–15ft (0.6–4.6m), to which the lure is tied. As the rig is dropped to the seabed, the boom stands out and keeps the trace from tangling around the mainline. When the flying collar rig reaches the seabed, the angler retrieves to impart action into the lure.

Bottom fishing

Many sea fish choose to live and feed on the seabed. The method used to target these species is called bottom fishing or ledgering. Fishing the seabed requires exactly the right amount of lead to hold the bait down, without moving, so a fish can find it.

One of the most simple bottom fishing rigs is the running ledger or running rig. A snap link swivel (or small boom) is threaded on the mainline to carry the weight and a short trace is tied onto the end of the line. Getting the correct type and size of weight in strong tides is critical to success. When the bait is taken by a fish, the snap link swivel on the mainline acts like a pulley, allowing the fish to run with the bait without feeling the resistance of the lead – until the angler strikes.

This lure is connected directly to the mainline using a snap link swivel.

A simple running ledger rig – this one is baited with peeler crab.

THE SEA ANGLERS'
FAVOURITE SPECIES

The cunning bass has achieved cult status because of its ability to challenge the skill and patience of the sea angler.

Bass

The sea bass is a favourable dish in many up-market restaurants. It is also one of the most sought after of all the ocean species and it has achieved cult status among British and Irish sea anglers. The bass is clever and cunning. When fishing for bass, the challenge comes in outwitting the species. The bass also fights well.

Location: Available throughout Britain and Ireland with the southwest counties of England and Ireland noted for exceptional bass fishing.

Favourite habitat: Shallow water and fast tides over rocky seabeds and sand banks. Also found in large numbers in estuaries.

Best months: May to October.

Top baits: Live sand eel, lugworm and peeler crab. Live mackerel can be good when boat fishing during the fall. Lures are great for bass fishing, too.

A good bass is anything over 5lb (2.3kg). Any bass over 8lb (3.6kg) is classed as a specimen fish.

Bream

There is no mistaking the ferocious, rattlelike bite and fight of the sea bream. There are several species available to fish, including the couch, gilt-head, red and the more common black bream.

Location: Black bream can be caught from all around Britain and Ireland but its cousins favour the warmer waters of southern counties of England, Ireland and west Wales.

Favourite habitat: Black bream can usually be found offshore in shoals over reefs and wrecks. Inshore, black bream can often be caught from many piers and beaches. The couch's and gilt-head bream are often found around the mouths of tidal estuaries and rivers, with red bream being a lucky find for the boat angler.

Best months: April to October.

Top baits: Rag worm, squid, peeler crab and shellfish.

There's no mistaking a bream when you hook one. Their rattlelike bites and ferocious fighting ability are unmistakeable.

Bull huss and dogfish

Bull huss and dogfish are small species from the family of cat sharks and they look very similar. However, bull huss grow much bigger in size than dogfish and they aren't as prolific. Dogfish, often a nuisance to anglers seeking other species, are one of the easiest bottom-feeding fish to catch. Aside from size, the difference between a dogfish and a bull huss is found by checking the mouths of the fish, which are slightly different.

Location: Both bull huss and dogfish can be caught from all British and Irish coastlines.

Favourite habitat: Bull huss favour rough and broken seabeds, whereas dogfish can be found in abundance over sand.

Best months: All year round.

Top baits: Mackerel, squid and any other strong-scented fish baits.

Some dogfish have hybridised with bull huss and form many mistaken claims for British records.

Cod

Cod is the British sea angler's favourite species and rightly so. This fish is big, fights hard and tastes great. Cod are present all year round, but in Britain there are several migrations. The most popular of these are the winter run of codling, which are caught from many beaches and the summer run of big cod, which tend to frequent offshore wrecks.

Location: Cod and codling can be caught

THE ULTIMATE GUIDE TO FISHING

Bull huss are a favourite fish for rock anglers thanks to their size.

from all four corners of Britain and Ireland. Cod is a much-pursued fish by sea anglers from Scotland and the north east.

Favourite habitat: Inshore estuaries and beaches during the winter. Offshore wrecks and reefs during the summer.

Best months: November to March for winter codling; May to September for big summer cod.

Top baits: Lugworm, squid, peeler crab and lures.

Cod are available to catch all year round. They fight hard and taste good, too.

Conger

Many anglers like to test their strength against the conger, because this fish fights tough and doesn't give up. The main reason for this is that the conger eel can actually swim backward and, with its strength and stamina, will often try to swim into a hole within the rocks to escape. Aside from sharks, the conger eel is one of the only big fish species in Britain and Ireland and many anglers will travel a long way to catch a specimen.

Location: Conger can be found around most British and Irish coasts. Very often, there will be conger eels lurking around submerged structures. The English Channel is renowned for massive specimen conger.

Favourite habitat: Around reefs, shipwrecks, and rocky ground.

Best months: All year round, but conger are more prolific feeders from May to October.

Top Baits: Oily and smelly fish baits, used whole, including cuttlefish, herring, mackerel and squid.

The British conger club qualifying weights are shore 25lb (11.8kg), reef 30lb (13.6kg) and wreck 40lb (18.1kg). Medal awards are bronze 55lb (25kg), silver 65lb (29.5kg) and gold 75lb (34kg). Each year conger weighing more than 100lb (45.5k) are caught by lucky anglers.

Flatfish

There are several varieties of flatfish available for British and Irish anglers, including brill, dab, flounder, plaice, sole and turbot. Dab and flounder are small flatfish, while brill and turbot grow well into double figures. Sole is another smaller flatfish species but one that is harder to catch. An unusual thing about flatfish is that their eyes and mouth usually lie to one side. In fact, it is possible to get both left and right-sided flatfish, just as people are right and left-handed. Turbot can grow to the size of rubbish bin lids. Many flatfish respond well to

If you're looking to land big fish, they don't come much bigger than the mighty conger eel.

Most boat anglers target flatfish such as brill and turbot.

Best months: Brill, dab, plaice and turbot — March to September; Flounder — November through February.

Top baits: Flounder and plaice — rag worm and peeler crab; brill and turbot — mackerel and sand eel; dab and sole — lugworm.

various attractors placed before the hook and bait.

Location: All British and Irish coastlines. The Channel Islands are renowned for great brill and turbot fishing.

Favourite habitat: Brill, plaice and turbot favour offshore sandbanks. Dab, flounder, plaice and sole can be found in estuaries and on many sandy and shingle beaches.

Ling

The ling is the largest and most prolific member of the cod family, but is eel-like in shape. It is also a deepwater species, meaning it cannot be targeted from the shore, only from boats.

Location: Ling are available throughout British and Irish waters, with the north east and the south coast offering greater quantities of this species.

Favourite habitat: Wrecks, reefs, rough ground.

Best months: All year round, although ling are more prolific feeders from May to October.

Top baits: Cuttlefish, mackerel, squid and lures.

Even though ling cannot be targeted by shore anglers, occasionally a rogue ling can be caught from the coast.

Mullet require finer tackle and more patience than any other sea fish species.

Although ling are very similar to eels in appearance, they are another member of the cod family.

Mackerel and garfish

Many sea anglers start life catching a garfish or mackerel from a pier. Both species are caught on light-float fishing tackle, which is a visual and exciting way to fish, especially for young anglers.

Location: Both garfish and mackerel are midwater and surface-feeding species and can be located around headlands and piers and from beaches. Mackerel are caught all around Britain and Ireland, while garfish are only common in southern counties of England, Ireland and Wales.

Favourite habitat: On the surface or up in the water where the tide increases or where the tide is broken by an obstruction, like a pier or headland.

Best months: May to October.

Top baits: Fish strip baits.

Mullet

Mullet are a specialist angler's fish and this is probably because they are believed to be a species of low edible quality, perhaps due to areas of dirty water where they are commonly found. For the sporting angler, however, the mullet puts up quite a fight. There are three main varieties of mullet: thick-lipped grey, thin-lipped grey and golden grey.

Location: Mullet are a migratory species, preferring warmer waters, so fishing is better in the southern half of Britain and Ireland, with the English Channel, Wales and southern Ireland noted for great mullet fishing.

Both Mackerel and Garfish have brought a smile to many anglers' faces and will continue to do so. Both of these species are often a sea anglers very first fish

Favourite habitat: Estuaries, piers and sometimes on the open coast.

Best months: May to October.

Top baits: Bread flake fished using coarse fishing tackle and tactics.

Pollack

The pollack is one of Britain's most prolific and widespread fish species. They are simple to find, simple to catch, they fight well and they are very similar to cod. Pollack are renowned for their heart-stopping run when first hooked and fishing for this species in the middle of winter can provide specimens in excess of 20lb (9kg).

Location: Pollack are available throughout Britain and Ireland. The English Channel is renowned for big pollack during the winter months.

Favourite habitat: Pollack love structures, including reefs, wrecks and steep coastal ledges.

Best months: All year round with November to May being the best months for big specimen pollack.

Top baits: Live sandeel, launce and lures.

From the shore, a pollack over 4lb (1.8kg) is a great fish to catch. At 10lb (4.5kg) and over, a boat-caught pollack puts up a tough fight.

Pollack are simple to find, easy to catch and they like to fight. These features attract many sea anglers.

Rays

Like flatfish, there are several species of rays targeted by the sea angler. These include blond, small-eyed, thornback and undulate. All rays are bottom-feeding species that are tough competitors, often hanging in the tide like a kite in the wind.

Location: Rays are found throughout Britain and Ireland with a fairly even distribution. Undulate rays are nearly always found offshore but blonde, thornback and small-eyed are targeted equally by both boat and shore anglers.

Favourite habitat: Blonde, undulate and small-eyed rays feed exclusively over sand or broken ground or offshore sandbanks. Thornbacks are different, preferring estuaries with discoloured water.

Best months: Thornback rays can be caught all year round. April to October are better months for other species of ray.

Top baits: Peeler crab, shellfish and prawn make excellent baits for thornback rays. Sandeels, launce and mackerel fillets are good baits for blonde, small-eyed rays and undulate rays.

Big sharks

There are several species of big sharks that roam British and Irish waters, including blue, porbeagle, thresher and mako sharks. Blue and porbeagle sharks are the most common and are regularly targeted by sea anglers. Threshers can be targeted, but mako sharks are generally caught by chance. Big sharks are only targeted by boat anglers.

Location: Porbeagle sharks can be found throughout British and Irish waters, with the tip of Scotland a great location. Blue sharks can be caught in the English Channel, along west Wales and from south and west Ireland. Threshers can be targeted in the English Channel from an area known as the "Five Mile Thresher Corridor".

Favourite habitat: Blue sharks are surface and midwater feeding fish that will often be found roaming warmer open waters in search of baitfish.

There are several species of ray to catch from around the shorelines of Britain and Ireland. Thornback and small-eyed rays are a favourite of shore anglers and big blonde rays are much loved by boat anglers.

Porbeagle sharks will feed on the surface, midwater and from the seabed and will often frequent reefs, shipwrecks and any other seabed feature while looking for food.

Best months: The warmer months of the year, when water temperatures are at their highest, are essential for blue sharks and thresher sharks. The porbeagle shark, however, is happy to live and feed in both warm and colder waters, so therefore it is a year round species.

Top baits: Large fish baits are essential when fishing for shark. These can be anything from a medium-sized mackerel, right up to a 5lb (2.3kg) pollack or cod. The art of attracting sharks is called chumming. This is where minced fish and oils are released into the water to attract sharks by appealing to their sense of smell.

Small sharks

Aside from dogfish and bull huss, there are three species of small sharks (sharks under 100lb; 45.4kg) that frequent British and Irish waters. These are tope, smoothhound and spurdog. Apart from the obvious – size – the main difference between big shark and small shark is that all the small shark frequent inshore waters as well as offshore. They can also be caught from the shore. There are two varieties of smoothhound – starry (with white spots across the back) and common (without white spots).

Location: Tope, smoothhound and spurdog can be caught throughout Britain and Ireland, from Scottish lochs to the west of Ireland and as far south as the Channel Islands.

Favourite habitat: Tope are often located around tidal races, headlands and other areas where there is a distinct increase in the speed of the tide. Both smoothound and spurdog are similar and prefer fast tides, but some cross underwater sandbanks and reefs.

Best months: April through to October.

Top baits: Mackerel is great bait for tope and spurdog. Hardback and hermit crabs are good bait for smoothhounds, but it is extremely difficult to get hold of these baits.

Small sharks such as smoothhound and tope are popular summer species. In some locations it's possible to catch both these sharks from the shore.

Big blue and porbeagle sharks are the largest sea fish species regularly targeted by sea anglers.

SEA FISHING RULES, REGULATIONS AND CONSERVATION

There are very few laws a British and Irish sea angler needs to be aware of. The coastline is free and no licenses are needed to fish the ocean.

Sea fish regulations and bylaws

Boats can be bought off-the-shelf and no courses are necessary to drive one. However, there are some regulations and bylaws specifically related to fish and fishing that the angler must be aware of.

Britain is divided into sea fishery areas that are run by committees and each area will have a list of fish species and local minimum landing sizes (MLS). MLSs are sizes given to fish species that have a commercial value, in which no one, by law, may remove a fish from the sea smaller than this size. Most fish are measured from the snout to the fork of the tail. As well as MLSs, some areas also have local bylaws that can restrict or prevent fishing or the collection of bait. Always check fish species MLS and for any local bylaws before fishing a new area.

In Ireland, fish are governed differently, especially bass. The minimum landing size is greater and no sea angler may kill more than two bass in any 24 hour period. Bass also have a closed season in Ireland, between the 15th of May and the 15th of June. This is to allow this species time to breed.

Sea fishing organisations

All around our coastlines and even inland, away from the sea, there are many sea angling clubs that have shore and boat fishing sections. Many of these clubs meet monthly in community buildings, clubs and pubs and are quite often named for the building where they meet. Most angling clubs are very welcoming and can be a wealthy source of knowledge for a newcomer to sea angling.

Many angling clubs will be affiliated to the all new Angling Trust. The Angling Trust is a single organisation that represents all game, coarse and sea anglers. The Angling Trust campaigns on environmental and angling issues and runs national and international competitions. They fight pollution, commercial overfishing at sea and a host of other threats to sea angling. The Angling Trust also promotes angling, developing programs to increase participation, particularly among groups who have yet to discover the joys of going fishing.

The Angling Trust is important to the sea angler as they are the only governing body of this sport, who aim to protect the rights of anglers to do what they love most – go fishing. Individuals, families and clubs are all welcome to join the Angling Trust.

Fish first aid

With today's sea angler becoming increasingly aware of conservation, the angler who plans to release his or her catch, either because there is enough for the table or perhaps it was just caught for sport, has a duty to care for the catch and to see that it is returned back to the sea in good health.

"Catch, photograph and release" is important to execute quickly. The longer a fish remains out of water, the increased risk that harm can be inflicted. Also take care of your catch in other ways. Try to use a landing net and choose one that is scale-friendly. Always use wet hands to hold a fish and avoid using cloths and other items that could remove protective mucus from a fish's body. If you must carry your catch back to where you are fishing, either to unhook or weigh it, do not let it flip and fall to the floor. A good idea is to use a net to carry your fish and, when unhooking, do not lie them on rocks. When weighing a fish that is to be returned, never hang them on your scales using the fishes jaw or gill cover and do not use plastic bags that could have contained harmful substances. Always use a weighing sling and soak it in sea water first. As you return your prized catch to the sea, hold it in the water and rock it backward and forward until it has regained its strength and swims away of its own accord.

When returning fish, handle them carefully with wet hands and do not drop them.

As you return your catch, carefully put the fish back into the water. Do not throw them into the water.

Hold your fish by the tail and rock it gently backward and forward to help the fish revive quicker.

When your catch has regained its strength, let it swim away when it's ready to do so.

THE ULTIMATE GUIDE TO FISHING

JOHN BAILEY
All images page 6–61.

HENRY GILBEY
www.henry-gilbey.com
Page 4/5; 7; 62/63; 64; 65; 66; 67 (both); 68; 69 (all); 70; 71 (all); 72; 73 (both); 74 (both); 75 (both); 76 (both);
77; 78 (both); 79 (both); 80 (both); 81; 82; 83; 84 (both); 85 (both); 86 (both); 87 (both); 88; 89 (both); 90 (both);
91 (both); 92 (both); 93 (both); 94; 95 (both); 96; 97; 98 (both); 99; 100 (both); 101; 102; 103; 104 (all); 106/107
(all); 108; 109; 111 (all); 112; 113; 114; 115 (both); 116 (both); 117; 118; 119; 120; 121 (both); 124/125; 126; 127; 129;
130 (top); 131; 133 (top); 133 (both); 134 (both); 135; 136; 137; 138; 139 (both); 140; 142; 143; 144; 145 (all); 146
(both); 147 (all); 148 (both); 149 (both); 150 (both); 151 (both); 152 (both); 153; 154 (all); 155 (both); 156; 157 (all);
158 (both); 159 (both); 160 (all); 161 (both); 162 (both); 163; 164 (both); 165 (all); 166; 167 (both); 168 (both); 169
(both); 170 (both); 171 (all); 172; 173 (top); 175 (all).

MET OFFICE
Page 128.

JIM O'DONNELL (FISHING GUIDE AND ANGLING JOURNALIST)
Page 130 (bottom); 141.

ANDY REES (MARINE BIOLOGIST)
Page 173 (bottom).